**CHATEAU**

1 – Cour d'Honneur
2 – Château
3 – South Wing
4 – North Wing
5 – Reservoirs

**PETIT PARC (former 'Jardins')**

6 – Parterre du Nord (North)
7 – Parterre d'Eau
8 – Parterre de Latone
9 – Tapis Vert
10 – Parterre du Midi (South)
11 – Parterre de l'Orangerie
12 – Bassin de Neptune
13 – Bassin des Saisons
14 – Bassin d'Apollon

**BOSQUETS**

15 – Arc de Triomphe
16 – Trois Fontaines
17 – Rond Vert (former Théâtre d'Eau)

18 – Etoile (former Montagne d'Eau)
19 – Obelisk (former Salle des Festins)
20 – Encelade
21 – Dômes
22 – Colonnade
23 – Salle des Marronniers (former Galerie d'Eau)
24 – Jardin du Roi (former Ile Royale)
25 – Miroir
26 – Bosquet de la Reine (former Labyrinthe)
27 – Salle de Bal
28 – South Quincunx
29 – North Quincunx
30 – Bains d'Apollon

**GRAND PARC (former 'Petit Parc')**

31 – Pièce d'eau des Suisses
32 – Grand Canal

**TRIANON**

33 – Forecourt
34 – Grand Trianon
35 – Parterres du Grand Trianon
36 – Bosquets de Trianon
37 – Petit Trianon
38 – Jardin français
39 – Pavillon français
40 – Nouvelle Ménagerie
41 – Jardin anglais
42 – Temple de l'Amour
43 – Belvédère
44 – Upper Lake
45 – Lower Lake
46 – Queen's Hamlet
47 – Farm

# The Gardens
## of
# VERSAILLES

# The Gardens
## of
# VERSAILLES

Pierre-André Lablaude

Architecte en chef des Monuments historiques,
chargé du Parc de Versailles et de Trianon

Preface
Jean-Pierre Babelon

Directeur du Musée et du Domaine national de Versailles
et de Trianon, membre de l'Institut

ZWEMMER

First published in 1995 by Zwemmer Publishers Limited
26 Litchfield Street
London WC2H 9NJ

Distributed in the USA and Canada by
Antique Collectors' Club Ltd
Market Street Industrial Park
Wappingers Falls
NY 12590
USA

ISBN 0 302 00659 1

Acknowledgements:
The author thanks Géry Baron, Roland Bossard, Alain Durnerin, Annick Heitzmann, Simone Hoog, Guy Kuraszewski, Ioana Lazarescou, Jean-Marc Manaï and Nadine Pluvieux

The author and Zwemmer Publishers would like to thank the following especially: Yves Breton, photographer, for his enthusiastic cooperation, and Pierric Jean, of the photographic service of the Réunion des Musées nationaux, for his efficient help.

Translated from the French by Fiona Biddulph
English translation edited by Diana de Froment
Designed by Maxence Scherf
Picture research by Catherine Berthoud
Typeset by Dominique Guillaumin
Printed and bound by Graphiche Alma, Milano.

Jacket illustration:
*The Promenade of Louis XIV seen from the Parterre du Nord of the gardens of Versailles*, Étienne Allegrain, circa 1688, detail

Endpapers: original map by Marc Dekeister

# CONTENTS

# PREFACE

In his prose poem, *Les Amours de Psyché*, 1669, Jean de La Fontaine extols the splendours of Vaux-le-Vicomte, deplores the brutal condemnation of their creator, Nicolas Fouquet, and then moves on to celebrate the new gardens of Louis XIV at Versailles. Like all his contemporaries the poet was seeking to win the young sovereign's favour but he chose to express his feelings about Versailles in a manner which went far beyond mere flattery.

Curious to hear their friend Polyphile's tale of Psyche's love, his three friends agree to accompany him on a walk in the country. They know how much 'he loves gardens, flowers and shady trees'. It is suggested that they 'visit Versailles and see the latest improvements. They propose to leave early in the morning and see the novelties first so as to leave time to stroll afterwards and hear Psyche's story. The party agrees and sets off the following morning. The days were still long, the weather fine. It happened last Autumn.'

On arrival the four companions hastened first towards the exotic attractions: the Ménagerie, which led to various reflections on 'artifice and the diversity of Nature, which toys with animals as it does flowers'. Then they visited the orangery, which proved that at Versailles the king was master of the seasons and the continents: 'How I love orange trees; how sweet their perfumes seem to me'. After a swift detour to see the château, the heat of the day was upon them, our friends went and sat in the Grotte de Thétis, where they were entertained for a while by the clever water tricks, always sure to make the bourgeoisie laugh, before retreating a little distance from the fountains to listen to Polyphile's story.

'The heat of the day having passed', they left the grotto and continued their walk along the parterre. Descending the slopes of the great axis they marvelled at the gentleness of the slope, and at the way in which the views unfolded before them. In this amphitheatre lined with evergreen shrubs, Latona triumphs over the sarcasm of the Lycian peasants thanks to the divine intervention of Zeus, who turns them into frogs. Further on, 'along a path as wide as it is beautiful, one descends towards two seas, of remarkably original shape', the Bassin d'Apollon and the Grand Canal. Fountains played all round them. Water rose and fell in plumes, in vapours, in clouds, while the allées, under the control of the great gardener, burst forth in stars in all directions, running to the furthest reaches of the land: 'Every road is an avenue in the kingdom of Le Nôtre'.

Such splendours inspire La Fontaine to produce some universal reflections on the greatness of the Moderns:

*Such loveliness was unknown in days of yore.*
*All parks were orchards in the time of our ancestors;*
*The orchards are turned to parkland: the skill of our masters*
*Can transform the gardens of the bourgeoisie into princely realms;*
*How they work royal parks into gardens fit for gods.*
*What they have planted will endure for a thousand years!*

In the remains of the now-redundant settings created for the elaborate festivities of 1668, the three friends listened to Polyphile telling of the loves of Psyche, who was delivered at last from the evil spells cast by her enemies. Thanks to the god of love, mortal beauty finally triumphed over the vengeful goddess Venus and was blessed with Pleasure, the fruit of her union with Eros. Were not the gardens of Versailles made for Pleasure? A voluptuous union of the bounteous gifts of Flora, Pomona and Bacchus, they were created to please the senses.

At the vanishing point of the Grand Canal the sun set in the limpid sky. 'I beg you to look upon that flaxen grey, the colour of the dawn, that orange colour and especially that purple, which cloaks the king of stars', cried out one of the four friends before hailing the coachman who was waiting to take them back to Paris in the moonlight.

We need to be reminded of the degree to which contemporaries appreciated the sensuality of the gardens in the early years, because the romantic movement revolutionized attitudes towards the gardens. It became fashionable to denounce the seventeenth century for mutilating and constraining Nature, for its dreary abstract lines and shapes and for subjecting the visitor to a simple, outdated and before long indecipherable mythological code.

Accounts of Versailles written between 1660 and '70 by La Fontaine, Mlle de Scudéry, Mme de Sévigné and André Félibien are the latest observations by contemporary thinkers on a constantly evolving and, to them, clearly understood work of modern art. Their profusion of lyrical prose paints a picture of all aspects of the gardens: staggered parterres, views, statues, fountains and bosquets, held together by the bonds of love and power which bind Man and Creation, in a microcosm created by Platonic philosophy, Augustinian theology and recent discoveries in cosmography.

The young king, lover, conqueror and master of the most beautiful kingdom in the universe, was the incarnation of humanity itself. Beneath a Christian heaven, face to face with the sun of the Greeks, he commanded, in its image, this area of nature which he had decided to shape to please every sense and which he laid before his subjects and ambassadors from neighbouring kingdoms. Louis chose to imprint the image of himself as demi-god in the garden where all was his, upon his own times and upon future centuries. His own physique convinced people of his power. He was a brilliant actor, dancer and horseman: Roger overcame the sorcery of Alcine, as he had triumphed over the Fronde and the nations of Europe.

Long before there was a château at Versailles, there was wild nature, the great outdoors, fresh air and from its earliest days to its last there was the ardent pursuit of the beast, the empire of the hunt. Hunting had decided a hypochondriac Louis XIII to settle here and had provided Louis XVI with a physical distraction from fatal political disquiet which endured right up until the sinister afternoon of 5 October 1789.

The royal estates were constantly augmented. From Louis XIII's first land purchases right up to the last years of the Ancien Régime, the surrounding villages, marshes and ploughed fields were annexed, increasing their size from 500 to 15,000 acres, not including woodland. All the great game forests were eventually incorporated into one huge hunting ground. Every morning the hunt departed for Marly, Saint-Germain or Meudon, in search of deer, hare and wild boar.

The first gardens, superimposed over Louis XIII's park, were the scene of the great open air *fêtes* of 1664, 1668 and 1674, publicized throughout Europe by engravers and writers, while the château remained no more than a modest manor house, which grew little by little, and was remodelled to provide indispensable services. The gardens, laid out according to Le Nôtre's design, dictated the plan of the great château as the open air *fêtes* permitted spectators a glimpse of its future rooms. The crossing of the great north-south, east-west axis determined the angle of Louis Le Vau's new façade, and the lateral parterres underlined the importance of the central building, unusually overshadowing gardens on three sides. It is conceivable that the position chosen for the Parterre d'Eau at the top of the site made the high terrace of Le Vau's corps-de-logis redundant, and may have prompted its replacement by the Galerie des Glaces.

A third initiative was taken simultaneously with the decision to make Versailles the seat of the court and of government. It was to double the size of the grandiose side parterres to the north and south, making it necessary for Jules Hardouin-Mansart to add the colossal North and South Wings which extended as far as possible to the rear, making the central part of the building project like a huge avant-corps. The gigantic façade presented the visitor who climbed the ramps of the Parterre de Latone with a uniform front which made it impossible for the eye to stray into the vernacular world of the town and its mundane duties.

The new city that was the palace of Versailles was thus designed in accordance with the space occupied by the garden and the park, subordinated to the exacting lines of a wooded half-star shape of vast proportions. Some kind of everlasting miracle has preserved the views and the horizons on all sides, and the ring of forest continues to act as a vivifying and protective screen. Beyond the poplars at the gateway to Saint-Cyr, framing the view of the distance, lies the plain of Versailles. It is still a rural area which runs along the banks of the Gallie stream, the modest and indispensable uniter of the valley which completes the Grand Parc.

Le Nôtre's genius did not lie in his ability to design 'embroidered' parterres for the delight of nannies and their charges — all his predecessors, the *brodeurs du roi*, had done that — or in having successfully applied the techniques and accidents of nature demonstrated in the gardens of the Italian Renaissance to seventeenth-century French gardens. It lay in having worked out what he could apply to the impoverished site, with scientific exactitude and a sure sense of the physical world, rather than what he could extract from it. In the final analysis, if Versailles lacked the superb natural geography of Saint-Germain, for example, it did at least provide the unlimited potential — albeit at a high cost — to transform uneven terrain into a series of spectacular perspectives by building a combination of terraces, ramps and flights of steps.

In spite of the criticisms expressed after the death of the old king, in spite of changing fashions, in spite of confiscations of land, alterations and replantations, the major features of Louis XIV's gardens have survived into the late twentieth century. Fountains and statues are in position and some bosquets remain. The Age of Enlightenment spared the gardens for reasons of economy rather than out of respect for the creation of a bygone era. It contented itself with adding subsidiary features such as the Bosquet du Bain d'Apollon and the Bosquet de la Reine, the Jardin français and Jardin anglais at the Trianon and the Queen's Hamlet, avoiding any major alterations to the existing gardens.

The unhealthy state of the plantations was already clear twenty years ago. The trees were plagued by old age, disease and eaten away by parasites. They were deformed, unstable and dangerous. We predicted that drastic action needed to be taken, a centenary felling, following the courageous example of Louis XVI in 1774-76 and the Second Empire and Third Republic between 1860 and 1883. It is Nature's responsibility to remind Mankind of the dues he has forgotten. The storm in February 1990 inflicted such damage to old and fragile trees that the inevitable had to be faced. It was decided to replant. In an effort to appease public opinion, prevent delay and manage the costs, the vast operation was planned over twenty years.

Pierre-André Lablaude, Architect-in-chief of the Monuments Historiques responsible for the park at Versailles, has been alloted the difficult task which must be carried out in an exemplary fashion because it affects the most famous garden in the world. The great sensitivity which he has displayed in his treatment of this key part of our damaged but still magnificent natural heritage has increased his knowledge of the gardens, their history and their geographical limitations of poor soil with boggy lowlands. He tells the story of the gardens of Versailles from their origins to the present day with much originality and great perception.

That he has been keen to argue for the validity of the project without attempting to conceal the flagrant contradictions it harbours is understandable given that he bears responsibility for the restoration. He must of course take into account the entire heritage of the past, as the doctrine of the Monuments Historiques instructs, but which past should he adopt? The successive stages in the reign of Louis XIV? The changing attitudes and creations of the eighteenth century? Or the great park of the nineteenth century with its shady walks? And once he has settled upon one or other, how does he implement his decision? How long will it take to produce the results which took former gardeners dozens of years to achieve? How can Nature be both accelerated and suppressed? How can one stop the seemingly endless growth of the great trees? They too will one day violate their boundaries and stretch their shady boughs out over the walks and the bosquets in triumph. In so doing they condemn to death all the layers of lower decorative foliage which have been so carefully cultivated in front of their trunks. There are no clear or categoric answers to these questions. Choice born of necessity is gradually replacing the trees, as the gardens envisaged by Le Nôtre are reinvested with youthfulness, imagination, vigour, brightness and the power to give pleasure. Hubert Robert and Richard Mique's eighteenth-century creations are also being taken into account. The beauty of Versailles will be enhanced by this new diversity, the exceedingly high quality of the workmanship, the breadth of the plans, and which must be maintained for the enjoyment of future generations. Returning to the words of La Fontaine:

*What they have planted will endure for a thousand years!*

JEAN-PIERRE BABELON,
Member of the Institut

*View of the château of Versailles
and the Place Royale*

Pierre-Denis Martin, 1722

# Introduction

Generations of visitors from Paris have first experienced Versailles as a series of straight tree-lined avenues with three vast axes converging majestically at the château. From these spreads the grid of smaller streets and three centuries have failed to fill out this sprawling network punctuated by little houses and apartment buildings or countless gardens. Its unfulfilled ambitions have left the town with an air of slightly sad, provincial charm, the indelible stamp of an artificial creation and of the endeavour which decreed that Versailles must be both the centre of the universe and a utopia.

At the fork of the trident from which the avenues spring lies the Place d'Armes, an imposing, slightly convex esplanade. Deserted off-season, it is burnt by the midday sun and swept by winter's icy blasts. Beyond, all vistas from the west converge on the palace, an insurmountable wall more than twenty metres high, an incongruous collection of buildings accumulated over the centuries, a jumble of stone, brick and slate stretching for nearly a kilometre from the end of the South Wing to the top of the Opéra crowning the North Wing.

Behind the monumental, screen-like façade, the horizon stops at the spiky silhouettes of statues lined up along the ridges of the roof. Dormer windows adorned with urns and other ornaments stand out against the sky, each one arresting the view, as though the roof were the edge of the universe the centre of which was behind the gilded gates in the Chambre du Roi. Nothing in the town gives us any clue as to the extent of what this massive structure might conceal. It is as though each ruler applied himself with the same single-mindedness and astonishing consistency to accumulating the different parts of this pile with the express purpose of hiding from the town and keeping intruders out of the secret paradise created in 1662 by a young king just 24 years old. Nowhere is one given a glimpse of the garden behind. Two side portals alone appear to the north and south. They are slim almost to the point of invisibility, their floors paved with oak blocks to deaden the thunder of coaches crashing up from under the building, hence the name Passages de Bois. Only then are you finally permitted to step through the mirror into another world, the garden, which is precisely symmetrical to, but totally different from, the space stretching out towards the town.

The first thing you notice is the space which contrasts with the preceding confusion, then a façade, the reverse side of the one which faces the town. Except that this façade is faultless, a wonderfully-proportioned glowing, golden cliff of Saint-Leu stone, articulated by traditional classical orders which envelop and unify the web of raised-ground floors, mezzanines and little rooms behind which is the almost trivial, utilitarian world of the inner courtyards. Above the trophies crenellating the attic storey are the clouds, high above the parterres and the bosquets (the square plantations of trees within the garden), reflected in the ancient window panes discoloured by centuries of filtering the sun, sometimes duplicated in the depths of the Galerie des Glaces or mirrored in the smooth waters of the Parterre d'Eau.

Town side and garden side, thus Versailles has two faces. The town side was the court's domain, par excellence, representing the king's power over his subjects and the nation. The garden on the other hand was chiefly dedicated to pleasure, recreation and enjoyment. Nevertheless, the garden also tells us much about the king's view of the universe and the power which he attempted to exercise over Nature. Power over the Nation, power over Nature; power garden, pleasure garden. Versailles contains within itself these harmonies and symmetries, as well as inconsistencies, the riches and ambiguities of which are revealed to us by history.

Versailles is therefore not only a palace, not only the Galerie des Glaces, the Chambre du Roi and the Chapelle Royale. It is also the Parterre du Midi, the Tapis Vert and the Bassin d'Apollon, the quincunx plantations and the bosquets. It is the whole park as we know it, with its pools and Grandes Eaux, its dwarf box parterres vividly decorated with salvia, its avenues of immaculate cone-shaped yews and paths punctuated by milk-white marble statues. Here a cosmopolitan selection of tourists, mothers and nannies with children, and athletes in tracksuits, all stroll in fine weather.

Then, after a while, a few more precise scraps of information come to mind. Names learnt at school, Louis XIV of course; Le Nôtre, undoubtedly; Mansart, possibly. Vague recollections of the sun motif and probably a rather caricatured vision of the 'French style' garden. But how many of the visitors who tramp down the gravel paths every year ask the central questions: can this garden still be as the Sun-King conceived it? Is it authentic? If it is authentic, how have the stone walls, the marble statues and the gilded lead fountains, not to mention the clipped box hedges, the curtains of trelliswork, the avenues and the bosquets of fully-grown trees, survived the centuries undamaged? By what miracle has wood become as eternal as stone, foliage as true as marble?

The myth of a miraculously preserved, unchanging Versailles, a symbol of the genius of French classicism, dies hard. Its praises have been sung by generations of artists, poets and historians. In our own times its image has been standardized by postcards, tourist guides, cultural films and art books. It is a gloomy, fake portrait, though, painted as if we were expected to believe that these chestnut trees which dust the pools with their autumn leaves really had been planted by Le Nôtre himself.

How has the myth been handed down? Who has ensured the garden's preservation and taken care of its upkeep and renewal? Which parts are original? How greatly has it been altered over the centuries and subjected to changing taste and reinterpretation? Taking the idea a step further, we must query the existence at a particular moment of an ideal point when Man, forgetting the inevitable passing of the seasons, could have either deluded himself or imagined that time stood still, that the garden was frozen at its apogee, fixed, like a painting at the moment when it enters a museum.

*Perspectival view of the château
and gardens of Versailles,*
detail of the view towards Choisy
and Saint-Cyr

Pierre Patel, 1668

# The Garden of a Huntsman

Versailles owes its existence to hunting. It is difficult for us to imagine how the princes of France could have been so attracted by the perpetuation, ritualization even, of the ancient predatory instinct, the cruel lust for blood, suffering and death, when they presided over a court of such refinement that it became the role model for all the courts of Europe. Hunting, though, was the only form of physical exercise, apart from fencing, deemed suitable for the nobility. With its frontal assaults and flanking manoeuvres, its feints and ambushes, it resembled the art of war and for several hours at a time masters and servants, men and horses, were thrown together in an inextricable tangle, violent and barbaric. The preserve of the aristocracy, it was also a manifestation of power. Contemptuous illustrations of be-wigged and powdered princes swaggering around the famine-ravaged countryside on fine horses often recur in the 1789 lists of grievances. Escorted by liveried grooms with hounds baying at their heels, they devastated tenderly nurtured harvests.

Hunting was the motivation behind the creation of the royal residence. Picture a little valley, like hundreds of others in the Île-de-France, framed by the wooded hillsides of Satory to the south and Chesnay to the north. A stream called the Galie runs through it between two ponds known as the Étang Puant, or 'stinking pond', and the Étang de Clagny, only to trickle away among the marshes and the reeds further to the west.

Farming is hard here. Only a few patches of cereal and pasture can be cultivated because the heavy soil is saturated with water. There is a small village with a ruined medieval manor, a muddy road, a little church dedicated to Saint Julien de Brioude and the handful of houses which make up the village of Old Versailles. Further on you come across the little hamlets of Choisy, Noisy, Saint-Cyr and Trianon, each with two or three thatched cottages and even a few windmills on the ridges.

However, the land, which belonged to the Gondi family, is full of game. There are deer, the noblest quarry of all, on the fringes of the thousand-year-old forests which cover the lands of Saint-Germain and Marly; hares and foxes on the edges of the fields, and waterfowl which come to nest in the rushes.

From the age of six Louis XIII came here on hunting expeditions with his father, Henri IV. Sixteen years later, in the summer of 1623, he was tired of the village inn, where he had had to spend more than one night on a bed of straw, after having been surprised by the onset of dusk too far from Saint-Germain to return for the night. And so the young king decided to build a more welcoming hunting lodge on a low hill several hundred metres from the village. A modest pied-à-terre with roughcast plaster walls was quickly built, comprising a four-room suite and a few bedrooms for the grooms.

The king straightaway became very fond of this humble place where he could make the most of his independence far from the influence of the queen mother, Marie de Médicis. A small estate was soon annexed to the property, comprising a parterre extended by a little park of 117 acres acquired from seventeen neighbours. This was doubled in size in 1632 by the acquisition of 167 acres and the purchase of the seigneurial land of Versailles in the Val de Galie, as well as the associated rights ceded by the Archbishop of Paris, Jean-François de Gondi, for 60,000 *livres*. The ownership of the land confirmed, the new lord of Versailles embarked on the building of a real palace which was to be much more comfortable than the plaster hunting lodge. A moated brick and stone building with a square courtyard at its centre and a slate roof, it took the master mason, Philibert Le Roy, nearly four years to build.

The façade of the main building faced west and had eleven windows which took in the view of the Galie valley. A bridge stressed the axis and spanned the moat to allow access to the garden, laid out at the same time as the re-

*Parterre of the château
of Versailles*

Jacques Boyceau, 1638

The west parterre with its 'embroidered' motifs, here probably exaggerated by the engraver, was laid out on the site of the present Parterre d'Eau, beneath the windows of Louis XIII's château.

building of the house. The plans for the garden were drawn up by Jacques de Menours, nephew and pupil of Jacques Boyceau de la Baraudière, gardener at the Palais du Luxembourg and one of the first theorists of pleasure gardens. Boyceau de la Baraudière probably played a part in the creation of the garden at Versailles. This is suggested by the appearance of a plan in his treatise on gardening, *Traité de jardinage selon les raisons de la nature et de l'art*, published in 1638. This plan shows an extraordinary design for the west parterre at Versailles, the same as the one which actually lay at the foot of the garden façade. It is one of the first examples of the flat 'embroidered' border known as *parterre de broderie*. It was the precursor of the great ornamental compositions of clipped dwarf box growing out of sand and coloured minerals, gravel, brick or crushed marble, which were sometimes surrounded by flowerbeds, and which became one of the most important features of the 'French style'.

De la Baraudière kept the characteristics of the compartmentalized design developed during the French Renaissance: the smallness of the central pool, the narrowness of the paths, the continuation of the tight grid patterns. He allows us a glimpse, however, of more innovative elements such as a terrace open to the horizon, instead of one enclosed by walls, and little diagonal paths which create the beginnings of radiating effects at their angles.

He distinguishes himself chiefly by the sheer exuberance of his foliate patterns and arabesques with interlacing volutes, drawn from the pattern books of ornamentalists and from the applied arts such as gold and silverwork, marquetry, embroidery, lace-making and bookbinding, originally alien to the often unpredictable rules of the plant kingdom. These features would be achieved on a spectacular scale by the skilled marking out of the squares with planting lines and stakes in tilled earth, from a drawing hardly larger than the hand, and at a cost of hundreds of hours of careful pruning carried out not with shears — the iron damages and whitens the leaves as they cut them — but manually, by picking out every sprig and leaf one by one, in order to guarantee that the tiny shrub flourishes in spite of the precision of the design.

The design of this 'modern' parterre nevertheless shows certain glances to the past, not least of which is the small but undeniable lack of symmetry in the various motifs in the embroidered compartments. Were they ever as perfect and as fine as they look in illustrations, more an exercise in the art of engraving than gardening? But it is still true to say that these four acres of terrace play a special role in the development of garden theory before Le Nôtre.

A second phase of remodelling began in 1639. This time the garden was in the hands of Hilaire Masson and Claude Mollet, author of *Théâtre des plans et jardinages*, published in 1652, renowned for his work at Fontainebleau, the Tuileries and above all, Saint-Germain.

The new palace at Saint-Germain-en-Laye with its majestic stepped terraces based on the Villa d'Este, designed in 1594, was the great point of reference at the time. With the exception of the parterre, the little garden at Versailles by Menours, Boyceau, Masson and Mollet was, by comparison, a rather minor affair. Its site, which was roughly square, covered more or less the same area as Louis XIV's later gardens, today's Petit Parc. Its concept was simple; a chequerboard cut through by a central aisle much larger than the others which followed the line of perspective from the west parterre on the axis of the palace. It was intersected in the middle-distance by two diagonal axes radiating from a second circular pool, and ended up at a third stretch of water, the Rondeau, positioned on a natural shoal which fed the Galie. This was on the same site as the later Bassin d'Apollon, one of the largest pools in the park in the middle of which is a statue of Apollo in his chariot.

Unlike Saint-Germain, with its monumental graduated parterres which needed expensive terraces, the garden at Versailles had no walls or stone steps. The garden followed the natural slope of the ground. The visitor's only option was to follow it down until he arrived at the edge of the marsh, at which point he had to turn round and walk back up to the château. There were few attractions or ornaments for the visitor apart from the three consecutive pools. Nevertheless, Claude Denis, the fountain designer, was able to pump water from the Étang de Clagny to create some small water displays.

A small château with a small garden and a small park, the project was undoubtedly low budget. Even if it was royal, it was almost identical to the dozens of country houses littering the plains and valleys around Paris which belonged to the bourgeoisie and the lower echelons of the aristocracy. This humble dwelling was nevertheless the most treasured possession of a shy king who took refuge here far from the splendour and cares of society, and who was to instil the same love in his son, the future Louis XIV.

The latter, who came to power a quarter of a century after the first building works at Versailles, always insisted that his architects and his gardeners showed an almost sacred respect for this modest house, of such little artistic merit, out of veneration for his father and the desire to affirm his legitimacy. This respect determined irreversibly the lines which future projects were to take, however elaborate they might become.

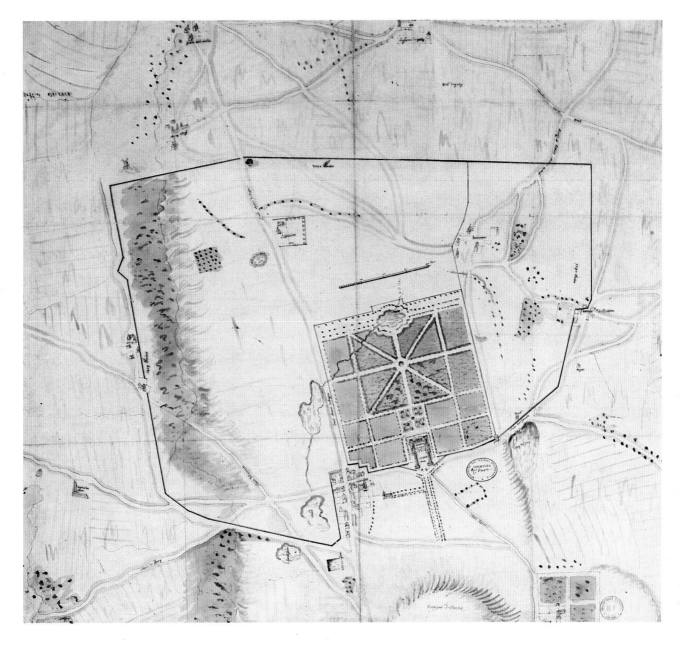

*Map of the park at Versailles,
the 'Bus map'*

Circa 1662

The garden designed by Jacques
Menours for Louis XIII occupied
the site of Le Nôtre's future
gardens. Abutting the village of
Versailles and bordered by the
ponds which connect up with the
Galie stream, the parterre, the
future Allée Royale, and the
quatrefoil Rondeau (on the site
of the present Bassin d'Apollon)
were aligned along its main axis.

*Louis XIV dressed as Apollo,*
*in the ballet* La Nuit

1653

# *The Age of the Royal* Fêtes

Every detail has been recorded of the sumptuous *fête* held in honour of the new king on 17 August 1661 by Nicolas Fouquet, Mazarin's treasurer and finance minister, at his new property, Vaux-le-Vicomte. Every detail has been recorded about this extraordinarily novel château with its great oval salon, its gilded ceilings embellished with sculpture, its splendid tapestries, its monumental vista and its terraced gardens viewed through jets of fountain-spray.

Not one of these details escaped the king's notice. On that hot summer day, Vaux-le-Vicomte appeared to him to be in a state of apotheosis. Never could he have imagined anything so magnificent. However, his wonder concealed mute indignation in the face of such extravagance, at so much money having been withdrawn from the nation's coffers with no holds barred. It concealed his jealousy of the impudent upstart, his nervousness as he began to realize how the finance minister was increasing his hold over the realm. But above all it concealed his wounded pride, as he remembered the little house at Versailles which his father had left him. He felt that he was no more than a prince among princes. Which one was the king today? His reaction was devastating and minutely thought out. Colbert had been carefully plotting Fouquet's downfall for months. Less than twenty days after the *fête*, Fouquet was arrested, accused of embezzlement, and thrown into prison.

Cultivated and ambitious, Fouquet was undoubtedly the first to have understood that a masterpiece of the scale of Vaux, the gardens in particular, could not be the work of one individual. That it had to be a concerted effort by ruinously expensive artists and craftsmen, gathered together, in a spirit of excitement, drawing mutual inspiration from each other's knowledge and talent. The team at Vaux was indeed extraordinary. Louis Le Vau was the architect, Charles Le Brun designed the interiors, André Le Nôtre created the gardens, Nicolas Poussin produced the decorative cycles while Michel Anguier did the sculpture. But there were also lesser characters, Robillard, who engineered the fountains, Villedo the mason, and a host of others who were to be found on the building site at Versailles several months later.

The year 1661 was the turning-point in Louis XIV's reign. It saw the death of

Mazarin, the elimination of Fouquet and the end of the seemingly interminable regency of the queen mother, Anne of Austria. This had become an increasingly heavy burden for the young king, who had come to the throne when he was only five years old.

The king's horizons cleared and the future was filled with promise when the Dauphin was born, ensuring the dynasty much earlier than had been the case for his father, two years after his marriage to the Infanta of Spain. Also passion flowered between him and his mistress, the ravishing Louise de la Vallière, whom he had set up in his Versailles retreat.

At Vaux, Fouquet had known how to shape a formidable creative team. Following in his footsteps the king partly dismantled the place, and took what he wanted in the way of men, furniture, chandeliers, tapestries, boxed orange trees, and nearly a thousand other trees. Vaux turned out to have been no more than a dress-rehearsal. Led by a new director, the following actors performed their drama, at first somewhat tentatively at Saint-Germain, and then more resolutely at Versailles.

According to the historian Pierre Verlet, the king 'loved architecture to the point where he reproached himself on his deathbed for having loved buildings too much. He was equally enamoured of anything to do with interior design. He took great pleasure in gardens, was very interested in flowers and enjoyed planting rare trees. His personal taste was reflected in the magnificence of Versailles. He was persuaded that a beautiful dwelling added as much to the glory of a great king as the conquest of a new province.'

He was a perfectionist; no detail went neglected. Dictatorial, he was inclined to take decisions without consulting others. His patchy education had left him with a preference for physical rather than mental exercise and an intellect guided more by a visual approach than an understanding of theory.

These character traits explain, in particular, his unquenchable thirst for drawings, maquettes and models which only had to receive his official seal of approval in order to be carried out. They also show his constantly changing mind on the site. Work which was hardly finished but considered insufficiently grand was immediately dismantled or demolished in order to be amended, to the despair of the designers, and in spite of Colbert's respectful remonstrations, as he counted the fortunes swallowed up by these aborted or constantly-changing projects.

Louis XIV was impatient. He wanted to see the work finished when it had hardly started, pestering the artists and forcing on the work. He wanted to see everything, make all the decisions, and considered himself to be the patron, the director and most important spectator of the work being performed all at the same time. He was only prepared to place his confidence in a limited number of intermediaries and, where the gardens were concerned, in two of Fouquet's artists from Vaux.

Charles Le Brun was one. Born in 1619, Colbert's protégé had been Premier Peintre du Roy since 1658, and was keeper of the king's collection of paintings and drawings. In 1663 he was appointed director of the Gobelins factory and he played a decisive role in developing the statutes of the Académie. Above all a painter, he worked on the great cycle *The History of Alexander* and the cartoons for the tapestries of *The History of the King* from 1665 to 1673. He oversaw the decorative schemes at Versailles: the decoration of the Escalier des Ambassadeurs, and the ceilings of the Grande Galerie, the Salon de la Paix and the Salon de la Guerre. He distinguished himself in the palace, as in the gardens, through his skill at management. As was written in the *Mercure de France*, 'All the arts work together under him'.

Le Brun orchestrated a considerable team of artists and craftsmen who created Versailles over the coming years. He specified the mythological and allegorical themes and designs for the fountains and groups of statuary, as well as the salons. He himself carried out the initial sketches from which the different employees worked and he oversaw the execution of painted, sculptural and architectural decoration. His drawings were exceptionally fluid, lively and dextrous, whether in charcoal or wash on buff-coloured paper, and must not be considered as mere virtuoso exercises, albeit by the most gifted artist of his generation. His work expresses an insatiable scientific curiosity about the living world and its metamorphoses. His animal sketches, studies of anatomy and human facial expression, are a rational and Cartesian expression of the relationship of the soul to the body, analysing and deconstructing the work of the Creator in the process.

Le Nôtre was the other. Born in 1613, he was 25 years older than the king and there can be no doubt that their difference in age, irrespective of the position which each held, was at the root of the almost filial rapport and trust that linked the younger to the older, the king to the gardener. Le Nôtre, however, was far from the simple bumpkin history has made him out to be — a modest colleague, devoted and talented, somewhat rustic, who refused the coat of arms the king wanted to bestow upon him in preference for that of which he thought himself worthy: 'three snails crowned by a cabbage leaf'.

*Charles Le Brun (1619-90)*
Nicolas de Largillière, circa 1686

*André Le Nôtre (1613-1700)*
Carlo Maratta, 1678

On the contrary, Le Nôtre was the pure product of a mid-seventeenth century scientific and artistic élite, the fruit of an intellectual ferment which, in a short time, turned all existing ideas about knowledge and creation upside down and established André Le Nôtre as one of the most original personalities of his age.

The son of a gardener and the grandson of a gardener, Le Nôtre was a legitimate member of a professional network which revolved around the Tuileries palace. His father, Jean Le Nôtre, was head gardener at the Tuileries and he and his family lived in the vicinity of the Pavillon de Marsan. This Parisian world, next to the royal parterres, looked onto unspoilt countryside to the west, through the middle of which the Champs-Élysées would soon be cut. Close by also were the royal workshops which had been housed in the Grande Galerie of the Louvre since Henri IV's day. Painters, sculptors, engravers and tapestry weavers lived cheek by jowl with clockmakers, mathematicians, engineers and architects, in an atmosphere of creative and studious ferment which fascinated the young Le Nôtre and determined his career to a great extent. However, his first love was not gardening but painting, and his early training as a painter took place in Simon Vouet's studio. Although Vouet painted the main figures in his many commissions, he had no qualms about entrusting his young students with less important or unrewarding work, including the preparation of canvases, mixing of grounds or the transfer of scale drawings to canvas. Vouet often went as far as to delegate the sketching in and painting of backgrounds, architectural fantasies and landscape settings for the central groups of figures to his more experienced students, as was customary at the time.

It was thus at Vouet's studio that Le Nôtre learnt drawing, how to sketch arabesques for the tapestry cartoons, practical geometry, theory of perspective and its optical illusions, the arrangement of planes, creation of depth and how natural scenery could enhance allegorical subjects. All of these skills were directly applied in the conception of the bosquets at Versailles. It was also at Vouet's studio, where he was able to study sketches of the antique and Roman campagna made by the master during a long stay in Rome, that Le Nôtre developed his ideas about landscape, formerly based exclusively on the countryside of the Île-de-France.

In the teeming corridors of the Louvre he acquired his eclectic education, a mixture of the artistic and the technical, of knowledge and of know-how, of understanding and of communication. During those long hours of study, when he practised working in a team, he made friends with the painters, sculptors and architects with whom he was later summoned to work.

He was 22 years old in 1635 when his father secured for him the position of head gardener to the king's brother and in 1637 he obtained a royal warrant which appointed him to work with his father until the latter's death. Whether as a result of atavism or family pressure, he too had become a gardener and it was in this field that he was to work at the Tuileries, Vaux, and finally at Versailles.

In those days the court was still itinerant. It travelled between the Louvre, Vincennes and Saint-Germain, Saint-Cloud and Fontainebleau. Sometimes it even stayed at Chambord. Versailles was still no more than one residence among many which the king happened to visit more and more frequently.

Taking into account the length of time it takes for plants and trees to grow, as well as the king's enthusiasm, the garden was laid out ahead of the building of the palace, which itself preceded the town. Work began in 1661 and successive plans show how rapidly the gardens and Louis XIII's little park were transformed in only a few years.

The costs were enormous. After two years they had already mounted up to 1,500,000 *livres.* The sum conveys the vastness of the undertaking, extended by the acquisition of land towards Noisy and Trianon, and parcels of land to the east towards the pump at Clagny and the village of Versailles, bought to allow for the development of a cross axis which cut through the courtyard of the little palace, on which two parterres were laid out. The northerly one followed the natural inclination of the hill and carried on into one of the first Allées d'Eau. The southerly one, known as the Parterre de l'Amour, was levelled, filled with flowers and supported by the the first orangery built by Le Vau.

Earth from the orangery made it possible to extend Menours and Boyceau's old parterre to the west. Its continuation below with a new composition completed the new Bosquet du Bois Vert. From 1663 the outlines of the gridwork crossed by diagonal lines appeared further on, to either side of the principal axis. These would become the twin bosquets, the Bosquet du Dauphin and the Bosquet de la Girandole. In 1666 the Labyrinth, to the south, unfolded its curved walks at whose junctions would one day stand 32 fountains illustrating Aesop's *Fables*, an idea attributed to Charles Perrault. Symmetrically, to the north, the first outlines of the future Théâtre d'Eau appeared (now the Rond Vert), as well as the completed Bosquet de l'Étoile, its paths laid out in the shape of a star.

Little by little, the garden was populated by sculpture. At first stone statuary predominated, followed by pieces made of more extravagant and durable materials. Among them, punctuating the high terraces of the two side parterres, were the bronze vases designed by Claude Ballin, the king's goldsmith (who created the famous silver furniture inside the palace), and the two marble sphinxes carved by Houzeau and Lerambert framing the western opening to the large west parterre. These were joined in 1670 by two gilded bronze child-riders, cast after a model by Jacques Sarazin.

These were the years in which the gardens of Versailles served primarily as settings for the festivities known as *fêtes*. The young king was the most genial of hosts. He loved dancing, music, carrousels and the theatre but there was also a serious message behind this frivolity. Performed in front of the entire court, assembled especially for the event, the *fête* was above all an exercise in prestige

*Louis XIV giving orders
to the master of hounds,* detail

Adam Frans Van der Meulen,
circa 1664

Seen from Satory, Louis XIII's
brick and stone château towers
over Le Vau's orangery and the
village of Old Versailles.

and charm, as well as being an assertion of the riches and power of the prince. The most famous of all these *fêtes*, 'The Pleasures of the Enchanted Isle', took place during a stay between 6 and 14 May 1664. It gave the court an opportunity to explore the latest improvements. Each day brought a new spectacle performed in a different part of the garden against backdrops masterminded by Vignarani. There were porticoes of foliage, architectural settings painted on canvas or gilded cardboard, shimmering with gold and fireworks, rooms which were sometimes enclosed, sometimes open to the sky, or which looked out onto the long vistas down the walks. Equestrian parades to the beating of timpani alternated with entertainments and ballets put to music by Lully, fireworks and ingenious machines, roundabouts of rings, races, jousts, lotteries and promenades. Three of Molière's plays were performed in the palace and the park on temporary wooden stages: *Les Fâcheux, Tartuffe* and *Le Mariage Forcé*.

The *fête* celebrated on 18 July 1668, on the return of the troops from the Franche-Comté and the signing of the peace at Aix-la-Chapelle, was probably the most splendid and certainly the most costly, at 117,000 *livres* for one day, that is to say more than a third of what was spent that year on work on the building and the gardens.

The July 1668 *fête* adopted the same general lines as that in 1664 but this time all the activities were packed into a single day. There were new temporary architectural settings and open air glades at the intersections of the paths. After a light meal offered to the court at the Bosquet de l'Étoile, guests walked down to the old Rondeau, where they were entertained by swans floating in and out of fountain spray before turning and walking back up the slope towards an amphitheatre set up on the site of the future Bassin de Saturne, one of the four pools dedicated to the Seasons. Here the most magnificent tapestries from the royal collections merged into the surrounding greenery. Twisted columns of false marble and lapis lazuli alternated with statues of Peace and Victory, framing a ten metre stage lit by crystal chandeliers. The canvas backdrop depicted an illusionistic view of the walk directly behind it, which led to the orangery.

Molière presented the first performance of *George Dandin* here in front of 1,200 spectators. The entertainment *Fêtes de l'Amour et de Bacchus* was also performed, written for the occasion in collaboration with Lully.

After the play supper was served, five courses each of 56 dishes, in a temporary salon put up on the site of the present Bassin de Flore, directly north of

*Seconde Journée*
*Theatre fait dans la mesme allée, sur lequel la Comédie, et le Ballet*
*de la Princesse d'Elide furent representez.*

*'The Pleasures of the Enchanted Isle',* fête *which took place in May 1664: a performance of the ballet* Princesse d'Élide

Israël Sylvestre, 1664

The second day's festivities took place in the centre of the Allée Royale, against a canvas backdrop painted to simulate the view looking back up to the château, thus linking the theatre to the garden.

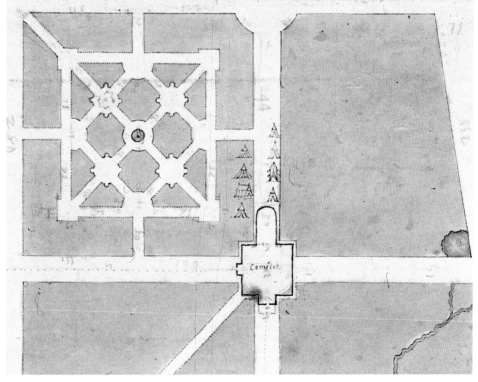

*Plan of the gardens of Versailles,* detail

Circa 1668

The theatre set up on the future Bassin de Saturne, for the 18 July 1668 *fête*, was accompanied by a series of tents which served as dressing-rooms and wings for the evening.

*View of the château of Versailles on the orangery side*

Israël Sylvestre, 1674

The old château with its tall slate roofs is no longer visible from the gardens. It has been covered by a new façade the chief feature of which is a great terrace in the Italian style but Le Vau's little orangery is still here, framed by the steps and the fir-lined avenues.

*Plan of the gardens of Versailles*

Circa 1668

This precious document shows the temporary architecture set up at the junctions of the walks for the *fête* on 18 July 1668. It also shows the precise state of the bosquets at this date, the Étoile to the north, the two central bosquets and the elaborate outlines of the Labyrinthe to the south. Thus it demonstrates perfectly the relationship between theatre and garden. The parterres are arranged around the château, which has been enlarged by Le Vau. The Parterre du Nord is dominated by the Bassin de la Sirène; the Parterre de l'Amour, adjoining the Bosquet du Bois Vert to the south, is supported by Le Vau's orangery.

*'The Pleasures of the Enchanted Isle', third day of the* fête, *7 May 1664,* detail

Israël Sylvestre, 1664

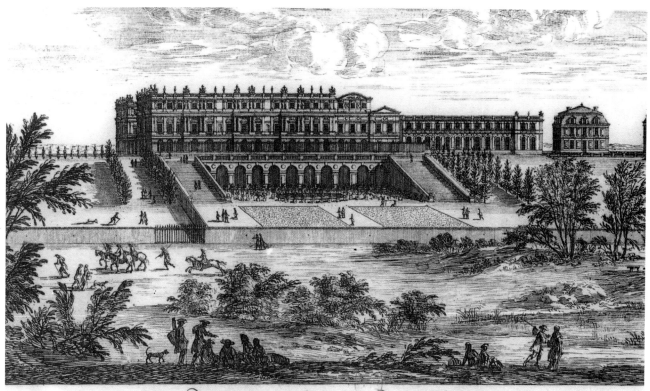

*Veuë du Château de Versailles du côté de l'Orangerie.*
*Fait par Israël Silvestre.*          *Avec privilège du Roy.*

the present Bassin de Saturne. This was followed by a ball held in an octagonal room designed by Le Vau. It was entirely decorated with elaborate rockwork and fountains, and the sound of the murmuring water mixed with the strains of the violins. As evening drew to a close the guests contemplated the gardens lit up by thousands of tiny lights, before the huge final explosion of fireworks and rockets outlining the king's monogram in the night sky.

These *fêtes* were remarkable workshops which allowed the king and his hundreds of artists, engineers and craftsmen to experiment with decorations which were made of wood and gilded cardboard, and then demolished the next morning. Thus they created a new formal and artistic vocabulary of effects which fell between theatre, garden and architectural design. These novelties often reappeared several months later, made more permanent in marble, bronze or newly-bedded plants. Finally, because *fêtes* imposed rigid deadlines on the workshops, they forced them to produce quickly and to the very highest standards. The *fêtes* therefore mark a definitive stage in the history of the gardens of Versailles.

*Perspective view of the château
and the gardens of Versailles*

Pierre Patel, 1668

The gardens are not yet perfectly
symmetrical. Placed around the
axis of the first château and
extended to the west along the
Galie valley, the Parterre du Nord
is on the right and the Parterre de
l'Amour and the Bosquet du Bois
Vert on the left. The buildings in
the far distance are presumably
the Ménagerie and the bell-tower
of the old church at Trianon.

# The Taming of the Natural World

The team was formed between 1662 and 1670. Le Nôtre and Le Brun were the first to be taken on. It is not easy to distinguish the work of Le Nôtre, often caricatured as a sort of green-fingered Jansenist, from that of Le Brun, trapped by his reputation of being a sycophantic and baroque decorator. The creative relationship between the two remains obscure and we do not know whether they worked together in harmony or in conflict. Nor do we know which one bore the brunt of the autocratic and perpetually disatisfied king, ever quick to redo work that had not even been completed; and the progressive ascendancy of Mansart, an opportunist of genius but one who only wanted to see a garden that was made of marble.

Over a period of 40 years the principles of garden design in the French style were going to be illustrated here in all their glory. A rigidly symmetrical composition was arranged around a main axis almost ten kilometres long, with parallel and perpendicular secondary axes. From the west parterre to the Grand Canal, graduated terraces were used to set up a cascade of fountains and pools, fed by a complex hydraulic system, linked by gravity. The garden was also characterized by huge amounts of architectural and sculptural decoration: grottoes, buffets d'eau, statues, vases, as well as a highly complicated system of pruning. There was pruning of vegetation into natural architecture, walls of greenery and decorative topiary, and also the hierarchy of heights and layering of the trees and shrubbery thus shaped into free or architectural form. However, the factor upon which Le Nôtre's contribution was really based, and that made Versailles unique, was the scale of the design, the sheer size of the project, the outrageousness of the creative ambition that it contained.

The medieval or Renaissance garden was an enclosed space, closely associated with its building, whether it was an abbey or a palace. It was like an island of civilization, of refinement and pleasure in the middle of a chaotic but above all hostile land. Under the influence of the Italian garden, the French garden was opened out into its surroundings by tricks of axial or lateral perspective which exploited the natural unevenness in the ground and made visual associations with the untouched or partly untouched nature beyond its boundaries. Le Nôtre was going to bring about a radical transformation of these early ideas. His first challenge was mastering a system of organizing the landscape into different stratas of planting on a site which was never intended to be developed so ambitiously. The first tier of parterres, a colourful, fragrant carpet laid out under the windows of the palace, led to bosquets with trees about thirteen metres high rising gradually to double or triple the height in the forested park behind. The whole composition swept towards the wooded slopes of Satory and Chesnay on the horizon, a gigantic amphitheatre unfolding as one left the palace behind and nature became more dominant, from the most extreme of architectural settings to the most rugged of natural surroundings.

The same scale is found in the rigour of the system of axes, which started at the palace, where the lines of the tight network of grids defined the square outlines of the bosquets, whose crossings radiated out in stars and *pattes d'oie*. They then seemed to take bites out of the horizon, becoming more and more dramatic as they turned from being garden walks into avenues for horsemen, forest roads, and the highways of the kingdom; bursting out one after another like a network of lines running all over the map, symbolizing the grasp of royal power throughout the country. Once it had been implemented, the scheme successfully conveyed a new and revolutionary global vision of landscape and space.

As a contrast to this web of axes, the project also used three interlocking pieces of land which began at the palace and went the entire length of the garden from the parterre to the hunting forest. The first piece was the Jardin, 93 hectares of parterres and bosquets enclosed by railings, known today as the Petit Parc, corresponding roughly to Louis XIII's garden, stretching from the façade of the palace to the Bassin d'Apollon. The second was the Petit Parc, now called the Grand Parc. It comprised 700 hectares and took in the entire width of the horizon visible at sunset. The third was the old Grand Parc, more than 6,500 hectares of semi-wild hunting territory, punctuated by the villages of Bois-d'Arcy, Saint-Cyr, Rennemoulin, Bailly, Buc and Marly. This was also a security zone, surrounded by a wall 43 kilometres long with 22 guarded entrances.

The garden had ceased to be an island, a refuge in the middle of a hostile world. It was in fact exactly the opposite. As a result of Le Nôtre's thinking and a Colbertian understanding of the economic and political function of

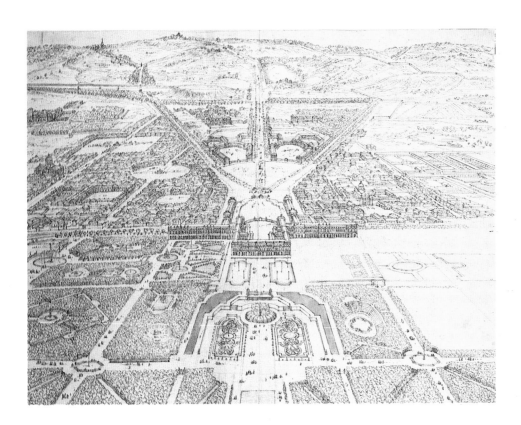

This bird's-eye prospect, a skilful theoretical exercise, adopts a viewpoint which the draughtsman could not have actually seen. The technique was learnt directly from Renaissance treatises on perspective. This new method of representation also had a determining effect on the appearance of the view itself, which can be seen, in part, at the beginning of the main orthogonal which is so characteristic of the French garden. It also expresses the relationship, patently obvious in Le Nôtre's work, between the techniques of the painter and the garden designer.

*View of the château and the town of Versailles from the Place Royale*

Israël Sylvestre, circa 1690

Versailles appears in a state of apotheosis. The two wings and the stables are on the verge of completion. The town is filling out. On the garden side, the construction of Mansart's large orangery has made it possible to double the size of the Parterre du Midi, and a dozen or so green chambers can be seen cut out of the wooded areas in the gridwork of the garden.

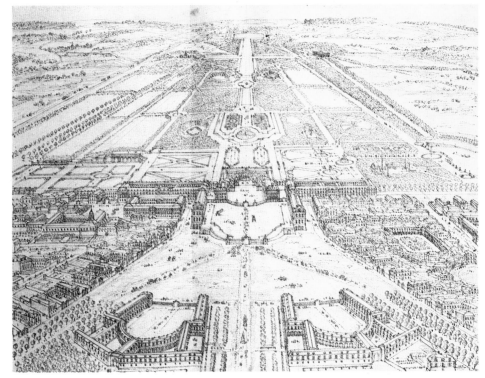

space, it had become the very heart and the driving principle behind a new kind of land management. Like a spider weaving its web, the garden was at the centre of a radiating mesh of channels furrowing through the forest. Soon converted into thoroughfares, these roads extended beyond the confines of the garden to the very frontiers of the provinces, dividing, classifying, organizing and exploiting the entire land. The dictatorial network encompassed the expansion of agriculture and the passage from primitive wood-gathering to real forest management. It helped travel, trade and commerce, and made it possible to control the resources of the provinces. By allying topography to the law of the land, the surveyor became the taxman's purveyor and thus the centralization of power was accomplished.

The garden represented order, culture in both senses of the word, civilization and power. It established a new relationship between Man and Nature. The mythical terrors of medieval chaos were now a thing of the past. The discovery of the New World, the new vision of the universe and the important advances made by science, were giving the men of this century a more rational understanding of the work of Creation. Feared until now, the workings of Nature finally seemed to have been made clear. Now it was up to Man, and the right of the first among them, to tame it for his own use, so that he could become the new deity, the equal of the gods.

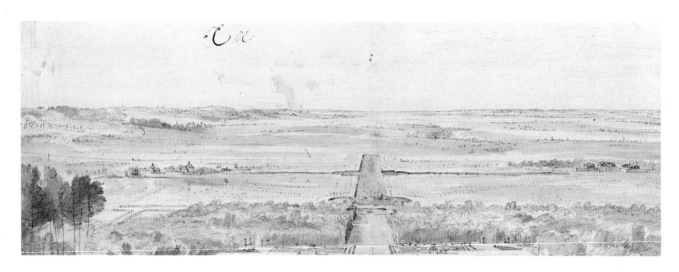

*View of the park at Versailles looking towards the west*

Adam Frans Van der Meulen, circa 1680

An expansive view of the Galie valley, seen from an upper storey of the château.

*Map of Versailles*

Early eighteenth century

The gardens unfold from the decorative parterres beneath the palace to the gridwork of gardens and bosquets. Beyond the beginning of the Grand Canal the framework of axes spreads out into its distinctive fan shape in a skilful play of radiating stars and perspectives, cutting through the woods and fields of the Petit Parc and running deep into the hunting routes in the Grand Parc.

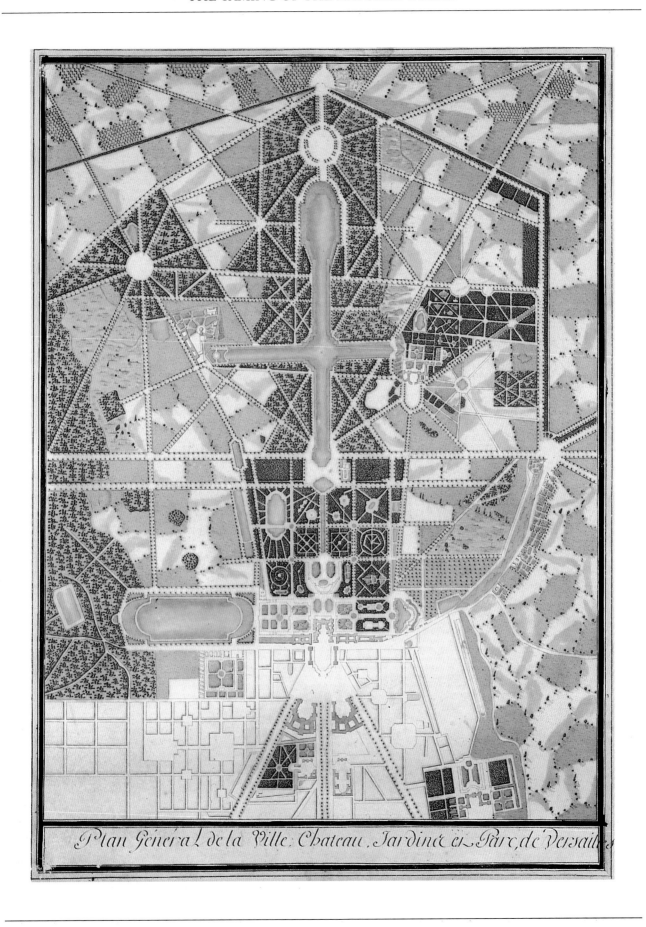

Plan Géneral de la Ville, Chateau, Jardins et Parc de Versailles

Louis XIV borrowed the emblem of the golden sunburst from his ancestor, Charles VI. In the process he deified himself through its association with Phoebus-Apollo. The sunburst became a recurring decorative motif, depicted in scores of ballets and sun masques, hundreds of them being fixed onto ceilings and wall-panelling in salons, and onto vases and gates in gardens. This celestial symbolism dictated the king's personal iconography inside the palace and out where multiple references to the story of Apollo, the solar cycle of the days and the seasons, could be seen. It culminated in the themes of the garden statuary, which drew heavily on Cesare Ripa's *Iconologia*, a sourcebook of illustrated allegories, translated from Italian into French and published in 1644. On his full accession to the throne, the king was at last able to 'govern by himself', obtaining complete power over mankind in the process. Fortified by this authority, boosted by the artistic and technical knowledge with which he had surrounded himself, Louis XIV decided to take on Nature.

The Sun orders the cosmos with his inflexible rules, but Apollo is also the god of harmony, the bringer of peace and the protector of the arts and sciences. The latter became the instruments of royal propaganda, the ideological discourse imposed on Nature and the garden, represented in the very place where absolute power was exercised and the king thus glorified. The royal wish to command the elements was distinguished by an ambition which, in the euphoria of his youth, knew no bounds. In relation to Nature this was expressed as a desire to enslave, not dissimilar to the subjugation to which the French nobility had been subjected by the Fronde, and the nations of Europe in the Spanish war of succession. Nothing would be able to resist the will of the divine monarch.

The king did not base himself at Versailles because the place lent itself to his aims but because the little house and garden in the marshy valley reminded him of his father. It was not the garden which determined the site, but the site which, in spite of its unsuitability, would be adapted to the garden.

The land which was to provide the foundations of the new garden needed considerable remodelling. The mound had to be levelled to enable the axes to be symmetrical and the belt of parterres even. On the town side it was necessary to dig through the hill at Montbauron which blocked the path of the direct route to Paris. Earthmoving, embankment cutting, excavation, transportation, muck-spreading, terracing, millions of cubic metres of earth were dug up with spades and pickaxes by men who heaved the debris onto their backs and loaded it into carts which dumped the debris several hundred metres away. Come summer, come winter, it was shifted, with the sole aim of pleasing the eye and creating symmetry. Thousands of pairs of hands were needed. Up to 36,000 workers toiled at the palace and in the gardens. Hundreds of horses plodded their way through the mud. It has even been said that people were killed or wounded, buried alive in mounds of fallen earth, run over by carts and wiped out by fevers.

The first orangery and the first parterres were not yet built on the same scale as stated in the Great Decree, launched after the 1668 fête. The aim of this decree was to create a new stone façade with terraces in the Italian style, which incorporated the old brick and stone palace on the garden side. Before long the size of the north parterre had been doubled, in anticipation of the radical new transformations. The size of the south parterre, however, was inhibited by Le Vau's orangery. The terraces necessary for its extention were

*Firework display on the
Grand Canal, 18 August 1674*

Le Pautre, 1676

Temporary architecture set up for
one summer evening on the Grand
Canal made a suitable platform
from which to launch
an elaborate pyrotechnical display.

not begun until 1678. This was an enormous job involving the removal of the lower parts of the Bosquet du Bois Vert, the raising of the ground needed for the upper extension of the new terrace, and the demolition of the little orangery. In 1681 a new orangery, designed by Mansart, was begun. Of cyclopean proportions, it was double the size of Le Vau's, and its 156 metre-long barrel vault, framed by the two majestic flights of steps known as the Cent Marches, formed a magnificent support for the parterre wall.

Undoubtedly the most thankless part of this giant reorganization was the dredging of the swampy shallows of the Val de Galie, a boggy zone carpeted with reeds, whose stinking smells and mosquitoes would have been intolerable beneath the windows of such a prince. The clearing of the marshes and their transformation into a vast lake resting on natural clay beds, later reinforced with artificial clay linings made it possible to drain the lower parts of the site. Masonry banks formalized the shapes of the lakes, allowing them to be incorporated into the general geometry of the park. Control of the water supply guaranteed that the lakes were kept free of weed so that the clear water could mirror the horizon in the distance and thus emphasize the depth of the axial perspective.

The excavation of the Grand Canal began in 1667. In 1671 it was extended, its shape branching out to the west in a star-shaped network of avenues which radiated through the forest in every direction, anchored by a transverse arm which gave it its definitive cross shape. By calling it the Grand Canal, reference was made to Venice, the mythical watery city. From 1669 the new Grand Canal was dotted with a fleet of miniature vessels made in various different arsenals around the kingdom. Some were even built in the dockyard set up at Petite Venise, a tiny, walled, naval town, placed at the east end of the new stretch of water in 1674. Brigantines lined with velvet and gold, feluccas decked with multi-coloured damasks, galleys and gilded gondolas chased away the ducks which used to nest here. There was even a miniature battleship, a royal vessel with pennants and flags decorated with fleurs-de-lys flying from its topsail, which lashed its way across this inland sea, bound for Trianon.

From 1678 a new stretch of water began to take shape to the south, at the Étang Puant, which collected drinking water for the village of Versailles. It was going to be a colossal mirror of water reflecting the new orangery, and the Swiss Guard was to build it. Part of the unit was even left behind in it, struck down by the miasmas of this unhealthy marsh, and by the utterly exhausting task of cleaning out its silt-laden mud. However, the Pièce d'eau des Suisses did not achieve its full size, twelve hectares, until Pierre Leclerc, the entrepreneur, had it dredged for a second time, in 1687. The remaining lake at Clagny was too off-centre to be incorporated into the garden's overall composition, and was therefore set aside for a different use.

It is very difficult for a gardener or garden enthusiast to contemplate still water and immobile reflections. Water should be lively and gushing as it is in Italian gardens, pouring out in a display of cascades, pumped from natural sources, flowing over terraces in a succession of fountains and pools in accordance with the theory of the *catena d'aqua* or 'chain of water'. It should bathe the passer-by in a fine vapour of droplets, deafen him with its thunderous jets and mesmerize him with its bubbling surface as he admires the infinite variety of its effects. But in this riverless countryside, devoid of any decent source of water, the great problem was how to provide it. Experiments were carried out with four different systems of supplying enough water to fuel the vast hydraulic schemes demanded by the king, who wanted water displays to be the chief ornament of his palace.

The first experiment adopted the idea of the pumping system at Clagny. It improved efficiency of the horse-power and a water tower was built, designed by Le Vau in 1664. This hugely increased the supply of water to the three clay reservoirs situated to the north of the palace, but also raised the height of the water level which now rose by means of a system of communicating pools, to feed a small upper reservoir, the Italian-style *casin*, created in 1665 between the pump and the palace, on the terrace of the Grotte de Thétis. This water reserve made it possible to bring water to the gilded sculptural group which adorned the Bassin de la Terrasse. This had been positioned as an ultimate refinement on the first floor of the palace in the empty space at the heart of the new garden façade which would subsequently become the Grande Galerie (now the Galerie des Glaces) begun in 1678.

But even the pump at Clagny could not provide enough water. Lesser springs on the slopes of Satory, Rocquencourt and Noisy had to be tapped along with all the marshland on the Glatigny side. New reservoirs, such as the three vaults under the west parterre, were hollowed out. Over several weeks an enormous amount of water would accumulate here, to be released in only a few hours for great water shows using up more than 12,000 cubic metres in

one day. All of Nature was called to the task of providing adequate water. Even the wind was set to work. A number of windmills were built: thirteen in 1682, at Clagny, Trianon and Satory, were equipped with six sails each to increase their power. However, they were never intended to mill grain, there was no longer any space at Versailles for barley or corn, but to turn their wheels to raise water from the lower springs in the direction of the Étang de Clagny. At the end of the line of pools and fountains, a reverse windmill even ensured that water from the Grand Canal was recycled, thus creating a closed-circuit system.

It soon became apparent that windpower was too weak as well as unreliable, and so it was to the water itself that Antoine Deville, a native of Liège, turned, when designing his Machine de Seine, an improbable and deafening mechanism built from 1681 on the Seine at Bougival by his compatriot Rennequin Sualem. However, even the Machine was far from successful. It was only used to supply Versailles for six months before it was limited to supplying the château de Marly.

A third system was tried between 1678 and 1685. Horsepower, windpower and waterpower had all revealed their limitations as well as those of pumping and raising techniques. Prospecting work to the south, by a civil engineer called Gobert, and the subsequent setting of the first topographical level by telescope by the astronomer and academician Abbé Picard, proved that Versailles was positioned slightly higher in relation to its plateau stretching from the Satory woods to Rambouillet. An upper network of pools was skilfully

*The Pièce d'eau des Suisses and the Parterre de l'Orangerie*

Jean Cotelle, 1693

The Pièce d'eau des Suisses, an extension of the Parterre de l'Orangerie, was an enlargement of the former Étang Puant, incorporated into the general symmetry of the garden. It collected water from springs to the south and was framed by four rows of trees which emphasized its semi-circular southern end backing onto the plains of Satory.

*View of the château, the gardens and the town of Versailles from the Étang de Clagny, detail*

Israël Sylvestre, 1674

Seen from the pond at Clagny the town and the gardens are taking shape, with (from left to right) the houses in the town dominating the four pavilions by Le Vau, the bell-tower of Saint-Julien, the water tower which pumped water from the pond and the château with its new stone façade. Also seen are the garden elements, the symmetrical bosquets of the Pavillon d'Eau, and the Berceau d'Eau flowing into the Bassin du Dragon on either side of the Allée d'Eau.

interlinked with channels and ditches which drained water from agricultural land into a series of pool-reservoirs contained by dykes. From here water travelled 34 kilometres through a canal system linking the pool at Saint-Quentin, via Versailles, to the reservoir at Montbauron. A parallel lower network of pools was driven from the south-west towards the valleys of the Bièvre and Yvette and the pools at Saclay, rejoining Versailles 45 metres above ground level through the Buc aqueduct, feeding the reservoirs at the end of the avenue de Sceaux. This system, the simplest in theory, the most accommodating

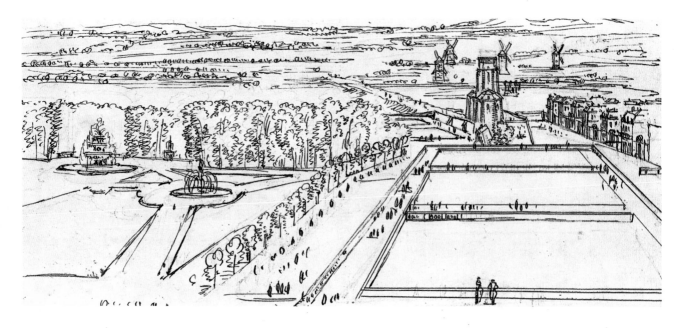

*The Parterre du Nord, the reservoirs and the pump at Versailles*

Attributed to Adam Pérelle, 1678-84

The view facing the opposite way, north, from the windows of the château, showing the design and the fountains of the Parterre du Nord, the low, geometric shapes of the clay reservoirs and, beyond the water tower, the windmills which raised water from underground springs for the Étang de Clagny.

*Windmill for raising water*

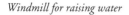

Seventeenth century

*Louis XIV and the Grand Dauphin on horseback, in front of the Grotte de Thétis*

French School, circa 1673

The countryside stretching out to the north shows the successive steps in the chain which led to the irrigation of the gardens, from the springs at the foot of the Chesnay slopes, the windmills and the pond at Clagny, to the water tower and pump, the walls of the clay reservoirs and finally, the upper reservoir on the terrace at the Grotte de Thétis.

of Nature, but also the most ambitious due to the length and complexity of its course, soon proved to be the most effective and operated for nearly three centuries. But even this, however effective, did not satisfy the king's ambitions.

He was on the threshold of an outrageous fourth project verging on megalomania. It aimed to re-route the River Eure, a tributary of the Seine, by connecting it to the artificial river formed by the upper chain of pools. Need-

less to say it was a resounding failure. In 1665 Gobert, Deville, the mathematician La Hire and even Vauban, brought on board by Louvois, were harnessed to this superhuman feat and the absence of a team of ancient Roman slaves was made up for by substituting the regiments of the Ferté and the Languedoc, Enghien, Champagne and Maine, 36 infantry battalions and six squadrons of dragoons in total. France was at peace and the soldiers were home from the battlefields. The campaign had some success in its early stages with the terraces and locks built across dozens of kilometres of canals along the river's new route. The project required, however, the construction of two gigantic overhead aqueducts, one at Berchères, near Chartres, and one at Maintenon. The second needed upper arcades 'twice the height of the towers of Notre-Dame', but only the lower level was ever built. It was with the acquaducts that the project foundered. The soldiers and workers were worn down by illnesses caused by the 'harsh work and the stink of all the churned up mud'. In 1689 the war of the League of Augsburg made it necessary to send the infantry back to the frontiers. The vast sum of 9,000,000 *livres* was squandered on this unfinished project of which nothing remained but the extraordinary silhouette of the first tier of the Maintenon arcades, a crow's-nest covered in ivy, like Roman ruins in a stage set, a bitter failure under the very windows of the king's new, secret wife.

The defeat sustained on the banks of the River Eure signalled the end of the dream of a Versailles perpetually animated by water displays. From now on water had to be carefully and parsimoniously meted out according to the timetables of miserly fountain controllers, who turned the water off as the king passed on his grand tour of the gardens, and on at the fountains he was about to discover an instant later at the turn of a walk, only to be thrown into a panic when he sometimes took an unforeseen route, either out of malice or by mistake.

Hundreds of kilometres of piping in stone, wood, cast iron and lead, hallmarked with the fleur-de-lys, threaded their way through the gigantic network of arteries, across the hills of the Île-de-France and the plains of Beauce. They were bound together by oakum and leather joints, buried underground or raised above. Across forests and valleys they went, with the sole aim of conducting the precious liquid to Versailles and distributing it through a multitude of fine capillaries drawn across the gardens. Here the skilful Francini, virtuoso descendant of a dynasty of Italian fountain engineers who had

*View of the Machine
and the aqueduct at Marly*

Pierre-Denis Martin, 1724

A series of fourteen paddle-wheels turned by the current activated a battery of 257 pumps which lifted the water up to the top in three successive stages by means of an ingenious interplay of rods and returns. From here the water was conducted along an aerial aqueduct, only to drop down by force of gravity towards Versailles, where it filled the reservoirs of Montbauron for the first time in 1685.

*Louis XIV visiting
the Montbauron reservoirs*

Jean-Baptiste Martin, 1688

The reservoirs, lined with clay and reinforced with masonry, were situated at the top of the hill overlooking the new town. Later on they supplied the new stone reservoirs, built as an extension to the North Wing of the château, whose maximal altitude supplied the pressure necessary to propel the highest water jets in the garden.

*Exterior of the
Grotte de Thétis at Versailles*

Antoine Le Pautre, 1672

The Grotte de Thétis was built
on the site of the Vestibule
of the present Chapel. Three
arcades with decorative ironwork
grilles and brass rods radiating
from a sunburst opened onto the
gardens. The grotto also concealed
an upper reservoir which fed
the waterworks and the Bassin
de la Terrasse, set into an open
loggia on the first floor of the
château. It was demolished
in 1684 to make way
for the North Wing.

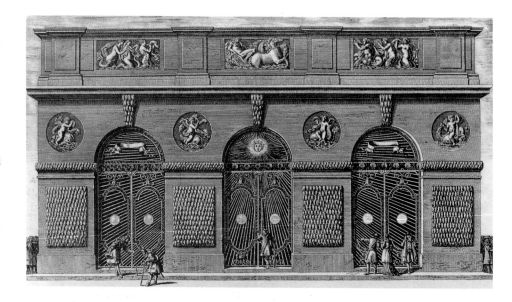

*The Grotte de Thétis and the
Bains d'Apollon*

Le Pautre, 1676

The surfaces of the interior were
encrusted with rockwork, mirrors,
shells and rock crystal, concealing
an infinite variety of water tricks.
Three large niches contained
the sculptural groups belonging
to the Bains d'Apollon.

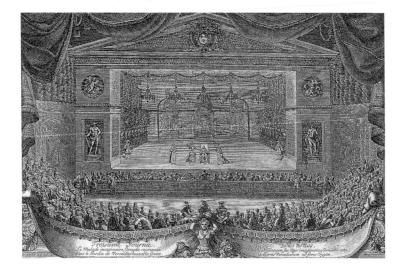

*The entertainments at Versailles
which followed the Franche-
Comté victory, third day,
19 July 1674;
a performance of the* Malade
Imaginaire

Le Pautre, 1676

The façade of the Grotte
de Thétis, swathed in foliage and
framed by temporary architecture,
provided a backdrop
for the evening.

come to France with Marie de Médicis, sculpted the crystal liquid into more than 2,000 different effects which splashed myriads of sparkling droplets onto the marbles and golds of the fountains. On evenings when there were fêtes, these plumes of water sometimes mingled with bursts of flames, gunpowder explosions or pyramids of fireworks, the fourth element of creation, even more fleeting and intangible, fashioned in the skies above Versailles by Torelli, the pyrotechnician.

Water displays were possible at the Grotte de Thétis, the palace of Phoebus-Apollo's wife, dreamt up in 1664 by the Perrault brothers to entertain the Sun-King and astonish Mademoiselle de la Vallière. Praised by La Fontaine in his prose-poem *Les Amours de Psyché et Cupidon*, this pavilion was the casket which concealed two splendid sculptural groups, Apollo attended by Nymphs and the Sun-god's horses groomed by the Tritons. Undoubtedly the most beautiful statues at Versailles, they had first been modelled in plaster and then carved in marble by Girardon and Regnaudin, Gilles Guérin and the Marsys, and set in position in 1676. The grotto married the arts of rockwork and hydraulics with a water organ and the mischievous play of water, which elicited shreaks and laughter from visitors as it surged up out of the ground unexpectedly or streamed over the rough surface of the vault.

Elsewhere water could be enchanting, as at the Bosquet du Marais, created in 1674 for the favourite of the time, Madame de Montespan, where hundreds of fine jets of spray squirted through reeds and trees with leaves of painted metal.

It could also be technically remarkable. Spectators at the Montagne d'Eau (now Étoile) and the Bosquet d'Encelade would catch their breath at the sight of the explosive violence of the enormous columns of water which erupted into the air. From 1685, the construction of new stone reservoirs which extended the old clay ones allowed the height of the jet of water at the Bassin du Dragon, redesigned in 1667 on the site of the first Rondeau du Nord, to be increased to 27 metres. Pools and fountains thus tiered the heights of the different jets which were often fed from inside by separate networks of pipes from a number of upper reservoirs and pools, also at different heights, or from various outlets fixed at varying levels in the great reservoir on the wing. Water was an integral part of the mythological theme, of the symbolic, one could go so far as to say political, discourse developed throughout the garden. At the summit of the great axis, the Bassin de Latone, created in 1670 and raised by Mansart in 1689, made a transparent reference to the vicissitudes of

*Diagram of a hydraulic calculation*

from *La théorie et la pratique du jardinage*, A.J. Dezallier d'Argenville, 1747 edition

The level of the upper reservoir determines the height of the jet of water reaching the lower pool through communicating vessels.

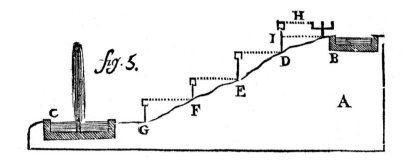

the Regency. It illustrated the story of the mother of Diana and Apollo, Latona, imploring Jupiter to avenge the mocking of the Lycian peasants, whom the lord of Olympus, in his fury, transformed into frogs. Meanwhile, at the other end of the Tapis Vert, the green stretch of lawn ending by the Canal, the *Chariot of Apollo* was placed in the centre of the Bassin d'Apollon. It showed Apollo leaving his wife Thetis's grotto in the morning and taking off on his daily flight across the heavens. The Sun-King himself reigned over the passing of time through the four statue groups symbolizing the seasons, *Flora* and *Ceres* to the north, and *Bacchus* and *Saturn* to the south, set up in 1673 and 1677, in the centre of pools at the crossings of the garden walks.

The most elaborate illustration of this quadrilateral symbolism was in connection with the new Parterre d'Eau, developed on the west parterre from 1672. Here the lobes of a quatrefoil radiated out of a central pool of water, their indented copings plaited with box, punctuated by bronze vases and marble statues. The Great Decree, passed by Colbert in 1674, commissioned 24 sculptors to illustrate six themes, each with four statues: the *Four Elements*,

the *Four Seasons*, the *Four Times of Day*, the *Four Quarters of the World*, the *Four Humours* and the *Four Poetic Genres*, and four groups of abductions. Plaster models were put up and later replaced with an initial series of sixteen marble statues, but the project was never finished. Designed to be admired from the first floor loggia of the palace, the parterre lost a great deal of its interest after the construction of the Grande Galerie in 1678. At ground level its sinuous and baroque lines could not be seen properly, and the statues had about as much allure as pallid skittles, ugly silhouettes which blocked the view. A radically new alternative, begun in 1683, was chosen instead. It was an idea of genius: to clear everything from the central axis, then nothing could interrupt the view of the horizon. One of the most expensive of the Francini brothers' ingenious creations, a remarkable effect was achieved by creating two huge new central pools. Water stretched all around, flowing from the highest part of the garden at the top of the hill, in two perfectly pure planes of liquid, rectangular mirrors reflecting the changing sky. Around their margins were broad rims of marble emphasised by a plain strip of grass. The composition was completed by male and female personifications of the four rivers of France, which alternated, pool by pool, with four nymphs and four children, leaning or lying down, so as not to interrupt the view. These statues were executed not in metal, gilded lead alloy or painted to look naturalistic, as was customary for the statuary around pools and fountains, but in bronze. Bronze was the most precious of materials because it was used for making cannons. This explains why the Keller brothers cast the statues at the Arsenal,

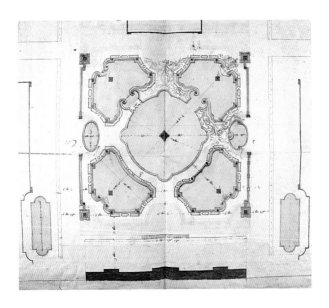

*View of the château of Versailles from the gardens*

Israël Sylvestre, circa 1680

The first Parterre d'Eau with its interlinking pools, urns, statues, fountains and topiary, unfolds beneath the windows of the Galerie des Glaces, framed by two groups of sphinxes (removed to the Parterre du Midi). This work epitomizes the taste developed by Le Brun, Le Nôtre and their circle during the first half of the reign of Louis XIV.

*Design for the first Parterre d'Eau*

Studio of Le Brun, seventeenth century

The drawing expresses the richness and the imagination in the different themes for the pools, the positioning of statues and the 'embroideries' in the flowerbeds.

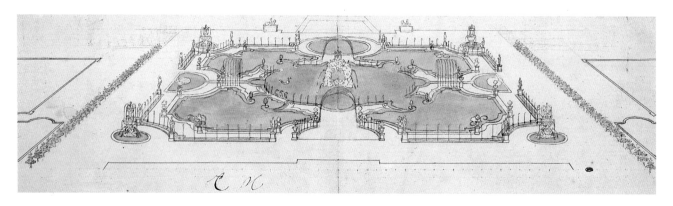

*Design for the first Parterre d'Eau*

Studio of Le Brun, circa 1674

Pictured as seen from the château, the fluid lines and curves of the water, shooting up in spears and sprays or raining down in vaults, complement the curving volutes of the pools framed by the verticals of the statues created by order of the Great Decree in 1674.

*Study of a fountain for the first Parterre d'Eau*

Charles Le Brun, seventeenth century

Although intended to be placed at the centre of different pools, these designs for highly decorative fountains were never executed.

*Winter*

François Girardon, terracotta maquette, after a drawing by Le Brun, circa 1674

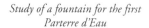

Le Lirique.    L'héroique.    Le Pastoral.    Le Satirique.

*The Four Poetic Genres*

Charles Le Brun, circa 1674

Inspired by the allegorical personifications illustrated in Cesare Ripa's *Iconologia*, these preparatory drawings were first modelled in clay followed by plaster, before finally being carved in marble.

### North fountain from the Battle of the Animals

French school,
seventeenth century

Although opposed stylistically, the two symmetrical fountains for the Battle of the Animals were contemporaries and neighbours of the Parterre d'Eau. Framing the view to the west, the rigid geometry of their marble pedestals and parapets was underlined by the rigour of clipped hedges and tall topiary the austerity of which reinforces the conventional perception of the style of Le Nôtre and the French garden.

CABINET
ES FONTAINES A DROIT.

### Design for a cascade

André Le Nôtre, 1684

In complete contradiction to the modern view that Le Nôtre's work was geometric and pure, rare signed works like this one for an unspecified cascade express a decorative profuseness and baroque exuberance which were highly influenced by Italy and are undoubtedly more typical of his taste than his actual executed work.

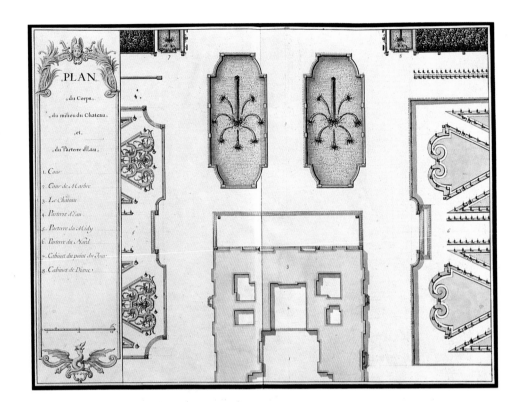

*Plan of the main body of the château and the Parterre d'Eau*

Jean Chaufourrier, 1720

The second plan for the Parterre d'Eau, work on which began in 1683, was a radical departure from its rich and complex predecessor. A pure and classical composition reveals a main axis framed simply by two symmetrical horizontal sheets of water.

between 1687 and 1690. They were undoubtedly intended to be gilded but increasing refinement of taste dictated that this would be too garish. Gilding was thus abandoned in favour of a natural patina which would stand out better against the sky and the façade of the palace, whilst recalling the verdi gris hues of the antique bronzes in the Vatican collections which were much admired by French visitors to Rome.

Three out of four of the abductions in the first project were, however, carried out. The first took its place in 1699 at the centre of the Bosquet de la Colonnade, followed by the others on the orangery parterre. The question was, what should be done with the series of 24 marble figures which had already been completed? Their symbolism ignored, they were dotted around the garden in an almost ad hoc manner, among the various statues which populated the walks and the bosquets: rare antique marbles from the royal collections, original works of art and copies by students of the Académie Française in Rome and, with a touch of poetic justice, the statues commissioned by Fouquet for Vaux, which the king bought in 1683.

We must turn to the aborted project for the first Parterre d'Eau to discover how these statues became no more than straightforward collectors' items, lined up on the edges of the north parterre regardless of their original allegorical significance, demonstrating how the sun theme was abandoned in the

1680s. *Autumn, America, Summer* and *Winter* stand on one side, facing the *Satirical Poem* and *Asia* and the *Heroic Poem* coupled with the *Phlegmatic*. Although they were designed to be seen as individual works in the round, the sculptures now stood in niches clipped into 'façades' along the hornbeam walks in the bosquets, whose tender greenery could not fail to enhance their immaculate whiteness.

The royal craving for absolute power, that 'arrogant desire to tame nature', did not limit itself to the four elements: earth, air, water and fire. The king wanted to be associated with the plant kingdom, the still more unpredictable world of the living. However, whether intoxicated by power or simply mad, the new demi-god's plans for the kingdom of Flora reveal many flagrant misunderstandings of the rules of nature, an overestimation of Man and even the king's abilities.

Thousands of old trees, elms and limes from Compiègne, beeches and oaks from Normandy, were torn up from the royal forests and transported in carts across the countryside, to the utter astonishment of Madame de Sévigné, who wrote that these 'forests of fully-grown trees in full leaf which are being brought to Versailles are replanted in conditions that are rarely satisfactory'. The results were catastrophic. The rates of survival were deplorable. Countless numbers had to be replaced as the king demanded endless aesthetic revi-

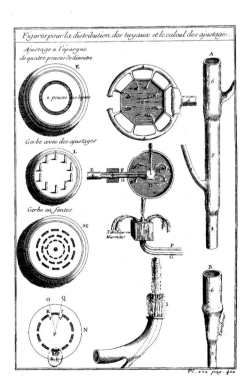

*Drawing for the Fontaine de la Pyramide*

Second half of the seventeenth century

*Diagrams of parts of fountains*

from *La théorie et la pratique du jardinage*, A.J. Dezallier d'Argenville, 1747 edition

François and Pierre Francini, the Intendants Généraux des Eaux et Fontaines, perfected a range of technical refinements in the science of hydraulics in order to maximize the number of different effects which could be created by water in the gardens of Versailles. With their complex networks of veins, ducts and arteries, they had much in common with recent discoveries in medicine and anatomy.

*Phrixus and Helle,*
design for an unexecuted fountain

Charles Le Brun,
seventeenth century

sions to the display. However, little by little and after years of technical and artistic fumblings, the desired effect was achieved, but the young elms and tender hornbeam saplings which managed to survive the uprooting and the transplanting were then tied down and submitted without mercy to the iron discipline of the pruner's shears. Nowhere but at Versailles could the art of pruning have been carried out on such a scale or been pushed to such extremes. Along the avenues and paths through the bosquets, there was no corner of the garden where one could escape from pruning in every imaginable form. Corridors of vertical *palissage* and horizontal ceilings created views or vaults cut back by gardeners as sculptors carve marble. The extraordinary curtains of hornbeam, elm and maple, clipped green walls with geometrically perfect proportions, planted in rigorously straight rows for hundreds of metres, rising to about ten metres, competed in height with Mansart's monumental walls. Topiary, so dear to Le Nôtre, was lovingly used to craft the most fantastic masterpieces, to confront the most famous sculptures by Tuby, Marsy and Girardon.

By imposing this rigorous geometric form on Nature's most fluid and fragile creations, water and trees, which are essentially free, and endowing marble and bronze, the coldest and most unyielding materials, much harder to work, with quintessentially baroque flexibility, Louis XIV undoubtedly created one of the most surprising paradoxes at Versailles, all to compel the awe and admiration of his subjects. As he entered this play of landscape directed by Le Nôtre, the first thing the pedestrian would see from afar was the sky. This was followed by the horizon and the leafy tops of the trees in the great park, the receding parallel lines of the perspectives cutting deep views and the cubic geometry of the upper levels of the bosquets. As he got nearer to the palace, he saw a succession of screens like the proscenium arches in a theatre. His eye was then drawn slowly down towards the parterres, hidden by the upper terraces overhanging them until the last moment, when at last his steps led him into the garden and he could see what was around him.

The garden was no longer something which bountiful Nature lavished upon Man. It had become something with which Man surrounded himself. Its quintessential expression was the parterre, half architecture, half garden, half artificial, half natural. The point is well-illustrated by the *broderie* technique with its outlines in relief based on Claude Audran's arabesque motifs and Boulle's marquetry; by the lawns bordered by high hedges of the Parterre du Nord; by the finer and more closely clipped silhouette of the Parterre du Midi, standing proud against its coloured mineral grounds, and by the individual pieces of turf cut into sinuous palmettes and the meandering steps of the popular Breton dance known as the *passe-pieds* on the Parterre de Latone and the Parterre de l'Orangerie. The garden's flowers were its crowning glory but unlike the orgies of colour we have inherited from the nineteenth century, the gardens at Versailles were planted with rare and precious bulbs, real collector's items. Worth their weight in gold, they were planted in vases or, more usually, lined up on open ground like rows of Chinese porcelain pieces or *objets* on the shelves of a dilettante's cabinet of curiosities.

However, the contortions which plants were made to perform were not merely exercises in geometry or formal virtuosity. They were also motivated by the desire to influence the times by importing and acclimatizing foreign plants, controlling the climate and the rhythm of the seasons in the process. The early years of the reign witnessed the generous use of the many different varieties of evergreens, such as evergreen oaks and firs, which were planted in the Bosquet du Bois Vert, or along the walks which framed the Parterre de l'Amour to the south or the semi-circular Bassin de Neptune to the north,

*Fontaine de Flore dans les Jardins de Versailles, representant le Printems. Cette Figure, et les Amours qui l'accompagne, sont de B. Tuby, du dessein de M.r le Br.*
A. Allée de l'Etoille .
B. Allée de l'Obeliste .
C. Allée sablée .
D. Autre Allée qui conduit à l'Etoille .
E. Allée qui conduit aussi à l'obeliste .
F. Allée qui va au bassin de Cerès .
G. Allée qui conduit à la grille de Trianon .

*The crossing of the Allées des Saisons: the Fontaine de Flore,* first state

Adam Pérelle, seventeenth century

The clipped *palissades* masking the smaller paths go round the circumference of the roundabouts, but allow access to the bosquets via the narrrow passages entered through the arcades.

*The crossing of the Allées des Saisons : the Fontaine de Flore,* second state

Girard, 1714

The English philosopher John Locke (1632-1704) marvelled at the 'sand-covered paths, raked every day, cut off from their counter-paths by walls of straight hedges no wider than half-a-foot or a foot, but green from top to bottom'.

*Examples of clipped yew on the ramps of the Parterre de Latone*

French School, early eighteenth century

'All of the yews on the descent from the Parterre de l'Eau to the Parterre de Latone and the lower parterre around the Latone are between four and five feet [1.2 and 1.5 metres] in height, and all of them were drawn from life'.

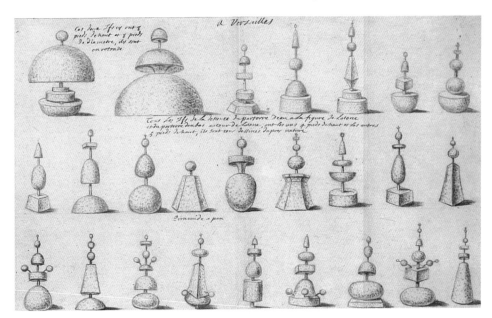

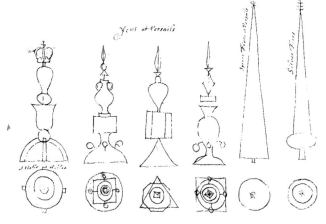

*Designs for topiary*

Alexander Edward, circa 1705

The art of topiary was unrivalled at Versailles. A wide variety of experiments were carried out to create new forms out of different species of trees and evergreen shrubs, including yew and box, holly, firs, pine and cypress.

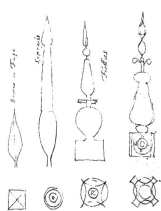

*Examples of clipped shrubs on the Allée Royale*

French School, early eighteenth century

'The variously-shaped clipped shrubs and yews on the Parterre de la Grande Allée Royale which descends to the Bassin d'Apollon are nine or ten feet [about three metres] in height. They are all drawn from life'.

spruce and yews, imported as seedlings from the Dauphiné region, and other varieties whose perennial greenery made it almost possible for the king to forget about winter altogether.

The passion for collections of orange trees, evergreen mediterranean shrubs, revived during the French Renaissance and after the return from the Italian campaigns. Seen at only the most distinguished of establishments, they were given preferential treatment at Versailles, where a special building, a veritable temple vaulted like a Roman basilica, was built to shelter an unrivalled miniature forest contained in 2,000 boxes during the winter months. The trees reemerged from the orangery in mid-spring and were set out along the parterre forming a south-facing square, where they were protected from crosswinds by the wings of the Cent Marches. They were also distributed around the park, bearing their sunny fruit, like golden apples in a new Garden of the Hesperides, along the paths where they alternated with marble urns. In mid-October they were returned to their winter retreat.

Ornamental plants were not the only ones to benefit from the control of the weather and the hijacking of the seasons. The new kitchen garden, laid out

*Plan for the Bassin de Cérès,*
second state

Jean Chaufourrier, 1720

A century after the plantations at Versailles had been laid out, William Chambers, the authority on the new landscape garden, wrote a critical essay denouncing the 'French manner'. He said he considered it a perverse confusion, neither town nor country, halfway between the path and the street, bosquet and building. He poured scorn on the claims that pruning was paramount and that not one single leaf must ever be allowed to flaw the perfection of the planting line.

*Map of the château
and the parterres*

Pierre Prieur, 1732

Originally designed to be viewed from the windows of the apartments, the parterres are arranged round three axes around the new Parterre d'Eau: the Parterre de l'Amour, then the Parterre du Midi, to the south (left), itself extended below the Parterre de l'Orangerie, the Parterre de Latone to the west (above) and the Parterre du Nord (right).

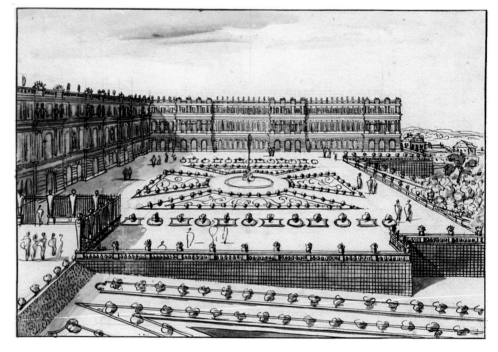

*View of Versailles,*
detail of the Parterre de l'Amour
and the Bois Vert

Pierre Patel, 1668

The flat expanse of the parterre
to the south was achieved with the
aid of the infill which supported
Le Vau's little orangery. It framed
the avenues of firs and backed
onto the glossy foliage of the
evergreen species in the Bosquet
du Bois Vert to the west.

*View of the Parterre de l'Amour*

Israël Sylvestre, circa 1682-83

This short-lived arrangement
around the Parterre de l'Amour
dates after the completion of the
south wing and before the
demolition of the first orangery.
Mansart's reconstruction
of the latter made it possible
to double the size of the garden
and form the new Parterre
du Midi in the process.

*Plan of the Parterre du Midi*

Jean Chaufourrier, 1720

The Parterre du Midi was originally composed entirely of 'compartments of embroidery and turf', whose dwarf box foliage stood out against coloured mineral grounds. The turf was not replaced by flowerbeds until the reign of Louis XV, on the insistence of the queen, Marie Leczinska, who could see the parterre from her windows.

*Plan of the Bassin and Parterre de Latone*

1747

Le Nôtre designed a monumental series of ramps overlooking the parterre. Built up out of remblai, they made it possible to view the cut-turf patterns and curved sandy paths from above.

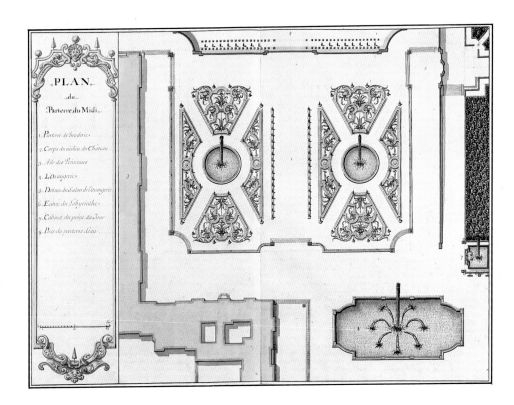

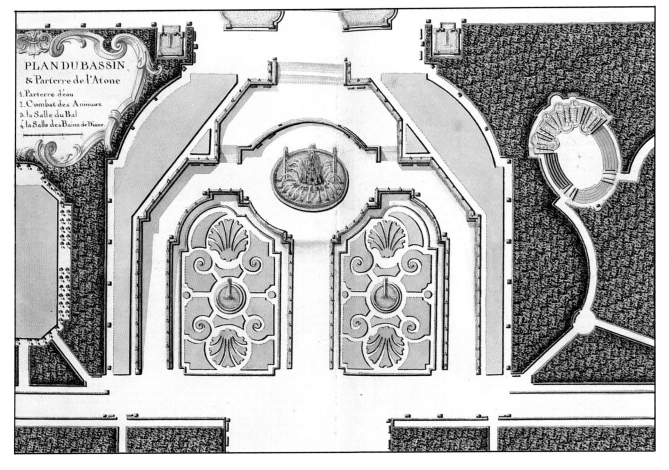

*View of Versailles,* detail
of the Parterre de Latone
and the Allée Royale

Pierre Patel, 1668

Laid out below the upper terrace,
the Parterre de Latone was
discovered as one approached the
garden. Framed by the clipped
walls of the bosquet, it had
patterns cut out of pieces of turf
and rows of topiary which
continued the whole way along
the Allée Royale.

*The Parterre du Nord*

Étienne Allegrain,
commissioned in 1688

The parterre was designed
as a series of triangular turf
compartments bordered by
flowerbeds punctuated with
shrubs and topiary. It unfolded

like a coloured carpet under the
windows of the Appartement du
Roi, continuing to the north by
the opening of the Allée d'Eau.
Behind it the observer saw the
tender green of the bosquets
which were still low enough to
afford a view of the wooded slopes
of Chesnay in the distance.

*View of Versailles,*
detail of the Parterre du Nord

Pierre Patel, 1668

A first parterre was created in 1663
at the foot of the north façade
of the château. Between 1663
and 1666 it was doubled to the
west. Using the natural slope in the
land, it was framed to the north
by the first walls of the bosquets
and by the three clay reservoirs
overlooked by the Grotte de
Thétis towards the town.

*Perspectival view of the orangery, the parterres and the château from the heights of Satory*

Étienne Allegrain, circa 1696

The second orangery, built by Mansart, backed onto the south flank of the gardens. Earth removed during its construction was used to expand the terrace of the Parterre d'Eau and extend it to the west by means of two ramps.

*View of the château and the orangery*

Circa 1700

In 1687 two of the sculptures known as the 'abductions' originally commissioned for the first Parterre d'Eau were added to the Parterre de l'Orangerie. The paths were lined with topiary.

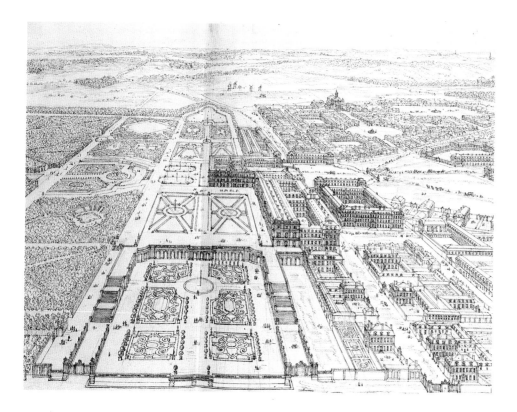

between 1678 and 1683 by Jean-Baptiste de La Quintinye who was director
of the royal fruit and vegetable gardens, replaced the earlier one created for
Louis XIII at the west end of the village of Versailles between the Étang Puant
and the Deer Park. Commited to providing fresh fruit and vegetables for the
king's delectation, it was planted on a barren site prepared with remblai from
the dredging of the Pièce d'eau des Suisses and covered with a layer of top-soil
from earthworks on Satory hill, enriched by massive quantities of manure
from the stables known as the Petite Écurie. The general layout of the kitchen garden, with buildings by Mansart, was designed to manipulate the climate and the time in which it took to ripen its produce.

Different methods of cultivation and technical procedures would be invented
and perfected here in order to obtain early fruit and vegetables as well as out
of season produce. Trailing fruit and vegetables were bedded-out *sur couches*,
in layers of compost in a hotbed. The heat produced by the decomposition
of the alternating layers of leaves and dung overcame frost and accelerated
growth. In 1685 the factory at Saint-Gobain began to produce glass on a
larger scale which encouraged cultivation under frames or in greenhouses
heated by wood-burners. The combination of these various methods made it
possible to serve the king's table with lettuces in January and strawberries and

*Emblems for the King's Tapestries,* plate 24

Paris, 1668-78

The 'pleasure garden' did not establish a hierarchy which placed the aesthetic, scientific and edible delights it lavished on Man in any specific order. The modern distinction between the ornamental garden and the vegetable garden or orchard was still quite alien. The miraculous products of the gardens of Versailles are evoked by the view of the orangery in the background.

*The kitchen garden at Versailles*

Aveline, late seventeenth century

Each square is enclosed by walls covered with espaliers against which different kinds of fruit trees were trained. The screens of masonry absorbed the heat of the sun and sheltered their precious produce from icy winds.

asparagus in March. This proved to the admiring court that His Majesty was truly master of the weather and the seasons. A building was even erected as a winter shelter for the 700 fig trees which produced the king's favourite fruit, making it possible to extend the harvest time to six months of the year. Louis XIV took a particular interest in his kitchen garden. He paid regular visits and learnt the arts of pruning and grafting, and experimental forms of agony inflicted on fruit trees to create bigger, finer and more succulent new varieties of fruit.

The king was Apollo incarnate among men. As he surveyed the water which he poured on his paradise, the forests which grew up in several months between his windows, the orange trees coming into blossom in his garden or the marvellous fruits, the result of his knowledge and his ingenuity, how could he resist the temptation of believing that he gave life to everything he touched? How indeed in the face of that circle of illegitimate children born by his different mistresses, that desire 'to see childhood all around', the cupids, the putti and little grotesques which populated the paintings and sculptures with which he had surrounded himself. How could he avoid giving in to the conviction that he was the embodiment of fecundity, and as monarch by Divine Right, God's own representative on earth?

The king's Ménagerie sprang from the same root. The zoo was begun in 1663, to the south of the Petit Parc, along the Allée de Saint-Cyr, at almost the same time as Louis XIV began to alter Versailles. By deciding to build a Ménagerie, the king perpetuated the ancient Roman princely tradition of collecting animals.

At the centre of the zoo, designed by Le Vau, was an octagonal pavilion topped by a slate dome. Around it ran a wrought-iron balcony which overhung radiating fan-shaped enclosures. Their entrances were framed by pillars in the form of carved statues personifying the zoological themes from Ovid's *Metamorphoses*. The Ménagerie welcomed its first residents in 1664, rare and exotic winged creatures, storks, pelicans and ostriches, followed by wild or dangerous beasts, after the closure of the Ménagerie at the château de Vincennes. These wild animals were acclimatized at Versailles in the Cour des Chèvres de la Thébaide, the Cour des Cerfs and the Cour du Lion. Elephant and rhinoceros, however, did not enter the collection until the eighteenth century. Although dedicated to scientific discussion and practice, from time to time the Ménagerie was used as an attractive little house with a central

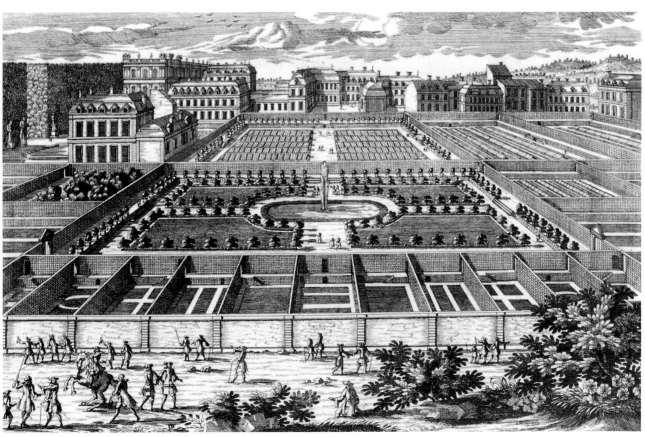

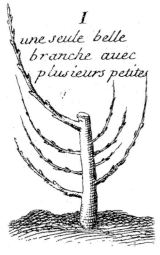

# I
## une seule belle branche auec plusieurs petites

# 3
## trois belles branches auec quelques foibles.

*Examples of fan-trained and espalier-trained fruit trees*

La Quintinye, from
*Instruction pour les jardins fruitiers et potagers*, 1716

La Quintinye was the director of the Jardins fruitiers et Potagers du roi. He attempted to form an advanced and undoubtedly excessive system of pruning the different varieties of fruit trees.

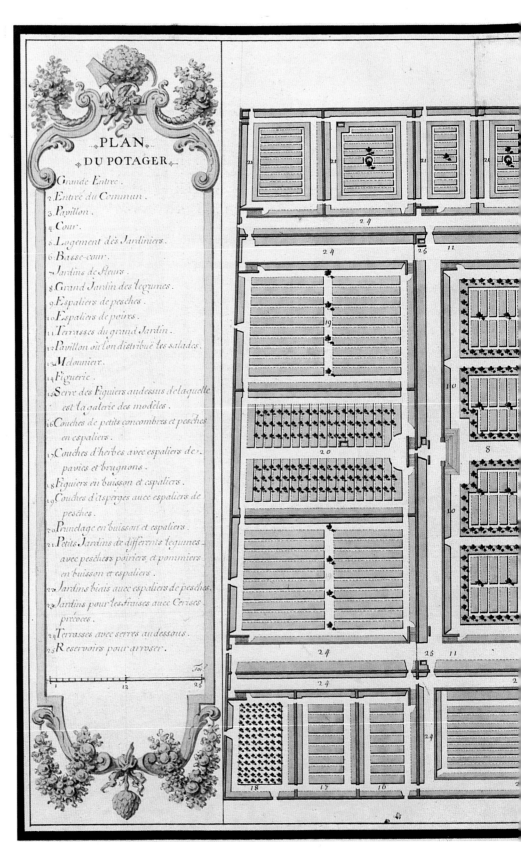

PLAN
DU POTAGER

1. Grande Entrée.
2. Entrée du Commun.
3. Pavillon.
4. Cour.
5. Logement des Jardiniers.
6. Basse-cour.
7. Jardins de Fleurs.
8. Grand Jardin des legumes.
9. Espaliers de pesches.
10. Espaliers de poires.
11. Terrasses du grand Jardin.
12. Pavillon où l'on distribuë les salades.
13. Melonniere.
14. Figuerie.
15. Serre des Figuiers au dessus de laquelle est la galerie des modéles.
16. Couches de petits concombres et pesches en espaliers.
17. Couches d'herbes avec espaliers de pavies et brugnons.
18. Figuiers en buisson et espaliers.
19. Couches d'asperges auec espaliers de pesches.
20. Prunelage en buisson et espaliers.
21. Petits Jardins de differents legumes avec pesches poiriers, et pommiers en buisson et espaliers.
22. Jardins biais auec espaliers de pesches.
23. Jardins pour les fraises auec Cerises précoces.
24. Terrasses avec serres au dessous.
25. Reservoirs pour arroser.

Jean Chaufourrier, 1720

The various vegetable gardens and orchards are designed around a rigorous framework of squares, planted low down and sheltered by overhanging earth terraces pierced by vaulted porches for wheelbarrows. The only exception was the 'slanting garden' along the main orthogonal, which was used for experimental displays facing north-east and south-west.

*A pruned fruit branch
in early May*

La Quintinye, from
*Instruction pour les jardins fruitiers
et potagers*, 1716

courtyard, a chapel, a pleasant cool room decorated with rockwork, fountains and ornamental parterres. It was also equipped with a group of outbuildings, a lower courtyard, a dovecote, a stable and a dairy, like a model farm. It even had its own kitchen garden. In other words it was a sort of miniature palace, a reduced-scale reproduction of the much more ambitious complex being developed simultaneously around Louis XIII's palace.

To get to the Ménagerie from the palace, visitors floated down the Grand Canal on a procession of gilded gondolas, their brocades dipping into the water, gliding along to the songs of the Venetian gondoliers and the strains of violins echoing from the surface of the water. Perhaps Louis XIV's guests sometimes wondered, confronted by the many marvels in this spectacle of Nature subjugated by the king, where water, trees, flowers, fruit and even animals each played their part, whether they themselves were really spectators or participants.

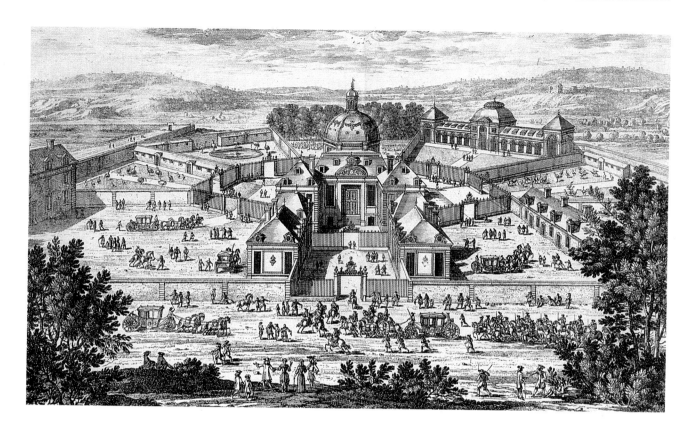

### The Ménagerie

Adam Pérelle, seventeenth century

Conceived by Le Vau as a sort of miniature château, the Ménagerie was designed around an octagonal, central pavilion whose upper storey afforded a panoramic view of the surrounding courtyards. In 1698 Louis XIV made a gift of it to the young Duchesse de Bourgogne, the wife of his elder grandson. Mansart created the Winter and Summer apartments, whose decoration made the Ménagerie seem more like a bijou country house.

*La Thorillière as Autumn, on a camel*

Preparatory drawing for 'The Pleasures of the Enchanted Isle', circa 1664

*Map of the château and gardens
of Versailles*

Israël Sylvestre, 1680

The first phase in the creation
of the bosquets lasted from 1661
to 1680. Fourteen different
compositions were inscribed
within the wooded squares
defined by the grid of avenues:
to the north (right) from
bottom to top, were the Arc de
Triomphe, the Trois Fontaines,
the Théâtre d'Eau, the Montagne
d'Eau and the Salle des Festins;
followed by the Bosquet du
Marais, the Dauphin, the Dômes
and the Encelade; on the other
side of the Allée Royale were the
Girandole, the Bosquet des
Sources and the Salle des
Antiques; finally, to the south
(left) were the Labyrinthe, the
Miroir and the Île Royale.

# The Pleasure Garden

The destruction, long ago, of many of the plantations and the closure of those which have been spared, now limits access to the gardens to the parterres and the main axes. Unfortunately this makes a visit to the gardens an incomplete experience not unlike visiting a château where you can only go round the hall and staircase without seeing the rooms.

Framed by geometric paths, the bosquets (also sometimes spelt 'bosket', the word comes from the Italian, *bosco*, and came into the English language meaning 'thicket' or 'shrubbery') in the Versailles style were enclosed on the outside by *palissades* of clipped foliage, surrounded by trelliswork. They were dense areas in which only narrow secret passages were found. Some were even covered over by leafy branches which created a vaulted effect. They lined the walks in a strict order only allowing visitors to discover the infinite variety of features behind them one at a time. It was as though they passed through the different sets of an opera as they continued along the route.

The bosquet was discovered from within. Paradise restored and a garden of the senses, it was designed to look like a real open-air chamber, a more concrete expression of the highly decorative temporary architecture set up at the crossings of the walks for the *fêtes*. However, instead of buffets made of wood and lampas, painted canvas structures and cardboard sculpture, there were polychrome marbles, wrought-iron or gilded lead. Here was a space ready-made for *fêtes*, balls and outdoor concerts. In that the garden took chronological precedence over the palace, the bosquets prefigured or complemented rooms inside the palace.

The first bosquets were planted at the same time as the early alterations to the garden and were rapidly followed by more complicated designs such as the Labyrinthe, planted in 1666, the Bosquet de l'Étoile in 1668 transformed into the more elaborate Montagne d'Eau in 1671, and the Théâtre d'Eau, begun in the same year. The first operation, conceived and directed by Le Nôtre and Le Brun, took nearly twenty years. It also included the Bosquet du Marais, to the north, the Pavillon d'Eau and the Berceau d'Eau, one on either side of the Allée d'Eau, redesigned six years later to form the twin bosquets of the Arc de Triomphe and the Trois Fontaines. Work continued to the west with the completion of the Salle de Festins, the Encelade and the Renommée, in 1675, balanced by the Allée Royale, the Galerie d'Eau or Galerie des Antiques and the Bosquet des Sources on the other side. To the south the scheme culminated in the Salle de Bal, a sort of outdoor ballroom laid out between 1680 and 1683. Forgotten here is the deadly rivalry between gardener and architect who collaborated over this enormous operation. The bosquets are the most perfect example of a true synthesis of two similar arts which mix and intermix extraordinary gardening, architectural and sculptural practices to the point where the enraptured spectator can no longer tell them apart. Reeds and trees fashioned out of painted iron at the Bosquet du Marais, turf benches inspired by the enclosed gardens and orchards of medieval convents at the Trois Fontaines and the Salle de Bal, triumphal arches made out of trelliswork and covered with jasmin and honeysuckle at the Encelade, topiary urns alternating with real gilded copper vases filled with ornamental shrubs, the smoothest marbles next to the roughest rockwork — it was all visual tricks, the art of illusion, of contrast and surprise, governed by similar decorative rules to those of baroque theatre. The most extreme example of this theatrical garden was probably the Bosquet des Sources, created by Le Nôtre in 1679 to the south of the Allée Royale. A rocky maze of serpentine paths threaded with countless streams, it was like a brief, fantastic, Mannerist sequence inserted into the garden's rigid grid, like a moment of discord intruding on harmony, creating a sudden, extravagant, atypical and unexpected confusion, to surprise the visitor and contrast with the immaculate order into which it had been inserted.

Le Nôtre is known for dividing chaos into neatly organized spaces. It is this side of his work which has been passed down over the centuries and which has earned him his reputation for rigour and austerity which can be slightly dull if it is not regarded as a precursor of Modernism. However, this work of parcelling out the land represents no more than the skeleton of his oeuvre, the meat of which — the bosquets in particular — has long since perished, like the bare ground of a painting whose surface has been stripped away by man or erased by time. The other, magical side, lost or hidden today, revealed the essence of his genius, culminating in the Bosquet de Sources. Here the artist had the strength to reintroduce discord into his harmonious composition by recreating part of the chaos he had originally found there, so endowing himself with quasi-divine powers at the centre of a universe which had already been completely remodelled by Man.

At this point we must avoid the traditional debate between the classical and the baroque, between a global, unified vision of landscape and garden, and the fragmented vision, playing on a series of contrasts; between two aesthetics defined with hindsight by our own century as two completely contradictory currents of thought but between which the artists of the period certainly saw no division. As a painter, Le Nôtre saw these two strands ultimately in painterly terms, like two dimensions of the same art, two complementary shades on the same palette, one of them beeing used for drawing the framework or the outlines, the other reserved for the surfaces, for modelling and for rendering contrast between the different motifs. The absence of the former can only detract from the latter.

The second phase in the planting of the bosquets came at the time of Le Brun's downfall in 1684, after Colbert's death and his replacement with a new team backed by Louvois. Hardouin-Mansart was mainly in charge and, though Le Nôtre was still the king's favourite, gradually extended his influence over the gardens to the point where he deliberately called into question some of his predecessor's creations.

In 1667 the Bosquet de la Renommée, finished two years earlier, was transformed into the Bosquet des Dômes, offering a taste of what was to come. Two white marble pavilions were put up and crowned with trophies and bronze and gilt-lead decorations. It was completed seven years later with the removal of the sculptures from the Grotte de Thétis, which had also been demolished to make way for the north wing. In 1684 the decision was taken to destroy the Bosquet des Sources, which had also only been finished for two years, in order to create Mansart's Colonnade. A work which could not be more different stylistically, the circular, white Carrara marble arcading of this magnificent open air temple stood out elegantly against a background of greenery. However, it was much criticized by Le Nôtre, who responded with the following unkind and ultimately unfair words when the king asked him for his opinion on the subject: 'Well Sire! What do you expect me to say? You have made a builder into a gardener and he has served you with a display of his own skill.'

However, Mansart's incontestable skill brought about a gradual change in taste. A more classical, more French garden aesthetic began to evolve, thus

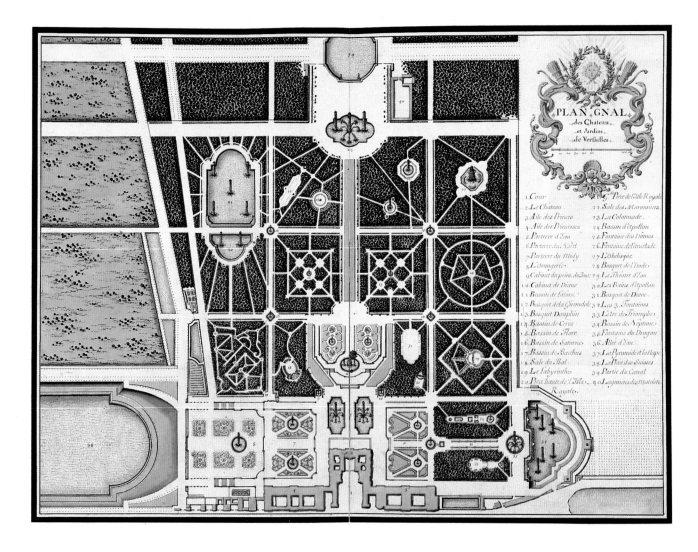

moving garden design away from the old theatrical Italian style. In total contrast to the work of the first gardening team, this new aesthetic introduced an increasingly marked distinction between masonry ornaments, now conceived as perfectly independent architectural objects, and their landscaped settings, which were to become just that. By doing away with trelliswork, using banks of grass instead of stone parapets, and cultivating lawns in the English style, the gardens were made to look more natural. There was a definitive break with that symphony of the arts, so brilliant and spectacular, whimsical even, occasionally on the verge of bad taste, that characterized the work done at Versailles during the early years of the reign of Louis XIV.

*Map of the château and the gardens of Versailles*

Jean Chaufourrier, 1720

This map shows the final alterations made at the end of the reign of Louis XIV: the Bosquet des Bains d'Apollon, to the west of the old Marais, the Salle de Bal, symmetrical with the longitudinal axis, the replacement of the Bosquet des Sources with Mansart's Colonnade and the transformation of the Salle des Antiques into the Salle des Marronniers.

*The Bassin de Neptune, the Bassin du Dragon and the Allée d'Eau*

Jean Cotelle, 1693

Le Nôtre dug out the Bassin de Neptune at the far end of the cross axis between 1679 and 1681. It collected the water from the upper fountains and produced a display of vertical jets of spray dominated by the terrifying spectacle of a column of water 27 metres high which shot out of the mouth of a dragon, carved by the Marsy brothers in 1667.

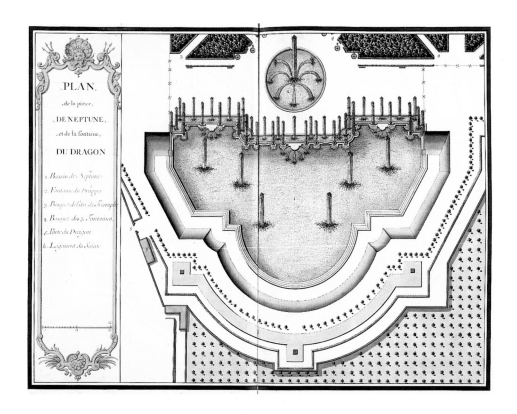

*Plan of the different parts
of the Neptune ensemble
and the Fontaine du Dragon*

Jean Chaufourrier, 1720

The Bassin de Neptune was designed like a theatre with a grass 'auditorium'. A mighty bank supported the 'stage' upon which an infinite variety of water displays were performed. Its fantastic allegorical figures and marine monsters in lead were not added until the reign of Louis XV and were heavily restored in 1889 for the centenary of the States General.

*The Fontaine du Dragon*

Jean Cotelle, 1693

The gardens of Versailles come into the château in the form of paintings when Louis XIV commissioned a number of artists to produce a variety of different views. The series of ravishing gouaches commissioned from Jean Cotelle in 1693 is the most famous. Enriched by allegorical scenes, each one is an accurate, and therefore very precious, portrait which can be used to identify the details of the gardens.

*The château of Versailles
from the Bassin de Neptune*

Jean-Baptiste Martin,
commissioned in 1693

Beyond the Bassin de Neptune and the Bassin du Dragon, the Allée d'Eau can be seen unfolding towards the Fontaine de la Pyramide and the Bassin du Bain des Nymphes. It passes the Fontaines des Marmousets as though telling the beads of a rosary, and frames two bosquets, the Arc de Triomphe and the Trois Fontaines, replaced by the more modest waterworks of the Pavillon d'Eau and the Berceau d'Eau in 1677.

## Plan of the Allée d'Eau

### 1747

The Allée d'Eau is seen in its finished state, sometime after 1688. Groups of topiary are set between fourteen round fountains punctuating two narrow strips of lawn. Eight similar fountains continue the series over the sandy area surrounding the semi-circle of the Bassin du Dragon.

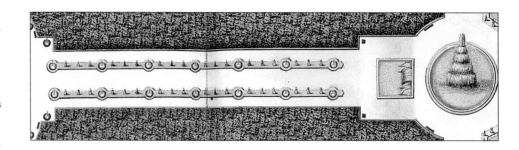

## Fontaine des Marmousets on the Allée d'Eau, group of Young Tritons by Le Gros

### Jean Le Pautre, 1673

## The Bosquet de l'Arc de Triomphe

### French School, seventeenth century

A green chamber is hollowed out of the interior of the wood and surrounded by a *palissade* with clipped niches. Its upper section has three *buffets d'eau* flanked by four obelisks. Its lower section is reached by a flight of steps and has three sculptural groups.

## The southern end of the Bosquet de l'Arc de Triomphe

### Jean Cotelle, 1693

This bosquet inspired awe primarily through its sumptuous materials and decorations: buffets and pedestals carved out of polychrome marbles, the triumphal arch and obelisks of gilded ironwork. It used and mixed the motifs and materials of architecture, decoration and metalwork and played with scale, substituting gilt-iron for gilt-bronze and rock crystal for water, for example.

The water display arched over the walk so that the promenader could pass underneath without being touched by a single droplet.

*The Bosquet des Trois Fontaines*

Jean Cotelle,
commissioned in 1688

Laid out by Le Nôtre and the Francini brothers according to 'the king's design', this bosquet replaced the Berceau d'Eau in 1677. It took the form of three terraces linked by sloping esplanades, cascades and flights of steps. Each of its three respective pools had a different shape: round, square and octagonal, and gushed jets in three different forms: the spear, the vault and the spray. Completely devoid of sculptural decoration, its natural and simple design was highly distinctive.

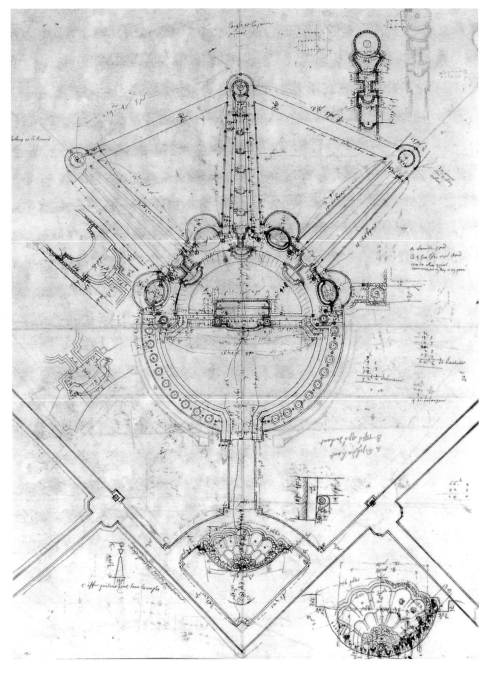

*The Théâtre d'Eau*

Seventeenth or eighteenth century

This bosquet, created under the supervision of the decorator Carlo Vignarani, introduced the architecture of the theatre to the garden. His circular design was divided into a 'parterre' framed by tiers of lawn and a raised 'stage' with a series of radiating views.

*The Bosquet du Théâtre d'Eau*

Jean Cotelle, 1693

The Théâtre d'Eau united the talents of an exceptional team of artists and technicians: Le Nôtre, Le Brun, Vignarani, the Francini brothers, the fountain engineer Denis and the sculptors Gros, Tuby and Gaspard Marsy. It also demonstrated the use of a wide range of materials including rockwork, millstone and shells, gilt-lead sculptures, earthenware and sheet metal vases, banks of lawn, trelliswork and topiary as well as countless water displays.

*Fountain design
for the Théâtre d'Eau*

Charles Le Brun,
seventeenth century

The allegorical themes which Le Brun selected for the garden ally and oppose men and animals, cupids and marine monsters in a variety of compositions.

*The Montagne d'Eau,*
*or Fontaine de l'Étoile*

Carolus Allard,
seventeenth century

This bosquet, situated to the west of the Théâtre d'Eau, was created between 1671 and 1674, and marks the centre of a star with five radiating walks. Its central pool contrasts marble edging with a mass of rough rockwork, and is surrounded by trelliswork niches overgrown with honeysuckle and crowned by faience vases. Simplified by Jules Hardouin-Mansart in 1706, its general outlines survive to this day.

*The Salle des Festins,*
*or Salle du Conseil*

Étienne Allegrain, 1688

Set up to the north-west of the gardens by Le Nôtre in 1671, the Salle des Festins was designed around an artificial island with four small pools at its angles. Promenaders crossed over via two revolving bridges. The green chamber was belted by a colonnade of alternating trees and topiary clipped into slender, tapering pyramids.

### The Salle des Festins

Adam Pérelle, late seventeenth century

Dozens of vertical jets of the same height, a simple hydraulic device, embellished the lines of the quatrefoil island and the parapet of its moat, emphasized by the lines of topiary.

### The Obelisk

Attributed to Martin, after 1706

Mansart erased the whimsical outlines of the Salle des Festins, replacing them with a more classical composition, with a central circle of metallic reeds concealing the ducts from which gushed the obelisk's 231 jets.

### The Bosquet du Marais

Jean Cotelle, commissioned in 1688

Madame de Montespan is said to have inspired this little bosquet, laid out by Le Nôtre to the north of the Parterre de Latone between 1670 and 1673.

*Detail of one of the* buffets d'eau *in the Bosquet du Marais,* elevation and cross-section

French School, pre-1704

The *buffet d'eau* was one of the features of the bosquets at Versailles. Precious vases were displayed on the graduated tiers of the buffet, over which rivulets of water flowed. Elaborately clipped hornbeam hedges reinforced the severity of the formal treatment imposed on plant and mineral.

*Central baldacchino, Bosquet*
*des Bains d'Apollon (maquette)*

Circa 1704

*Elevation design*
*for the new Bains d'Apollon*

French School, 1702-05

In 1704 Mansart replaced
the Bosquet du Marais with
a new design furnished with gilt-
metal baldacchini,
which sheltered the three
marble groups from
the Grotte de Thétis.

*The Bosquet de la Renommée,*
*later Bosquet des Dômes*

Israël Sylvestre,
seventeenth century

The figure of Fame is surrounded
by concentric balustrades in this
bosquet, composed by Le Nôtre
in 1675. In 1677 Mansart added
two white marble pavilions,
resulting in the new name.

*Sketch for the Fontaine
de la Renommée*

Charles Le Brun, seventeenth
century

*Plan and elevation of one
of the pavilions of the
Bosquet des Dômes*

Seventeenth century

Each pavilion is entirely made
of marble, decorated with bronze
and gilt-lead.

*The Bosquet d'Encelade*

Circa 1700

In the middle of the pool the
monstrous figure of the giant
Enceladus, who wanted to climb
up into the heavens to confront
Jupiter, suffers in agony beneath a
pile of rocks, spewing an enormous
column of water into the sky. A
charming vaulted trelliswork gallery
surrounds the octagonal clearing in
the middle of the wood.

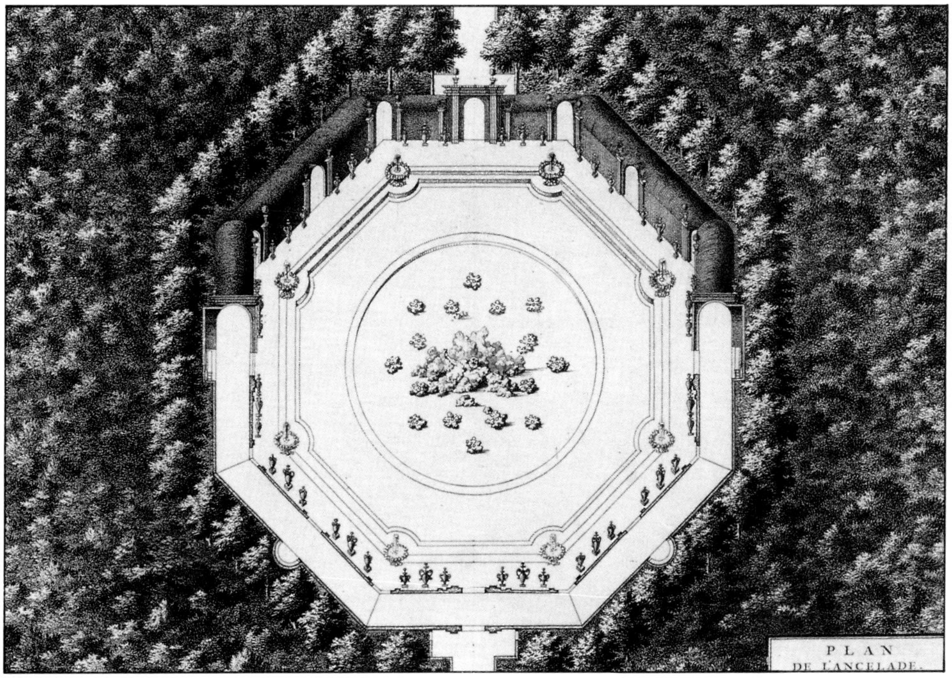


*The Bosquet d'Encelade*

French School, circa 1700

Its perimeter punctuated by triumphal arches, the arbour is adorned with scented plants such as jasmine and honeysuckle and contains topiary 'vases' as well as actual gilt-bronze vases bearing ornemental shrubs. The difference in level between the central pool and the trelliswork gallery is reconciled by a double bank of grass, marked at its angles by little rockwork fountains. In 1706 Mansart transformed the bosquet, sweeping away everything except the central pool, now surrounded by a slope of lawn and a hornbeam walk.

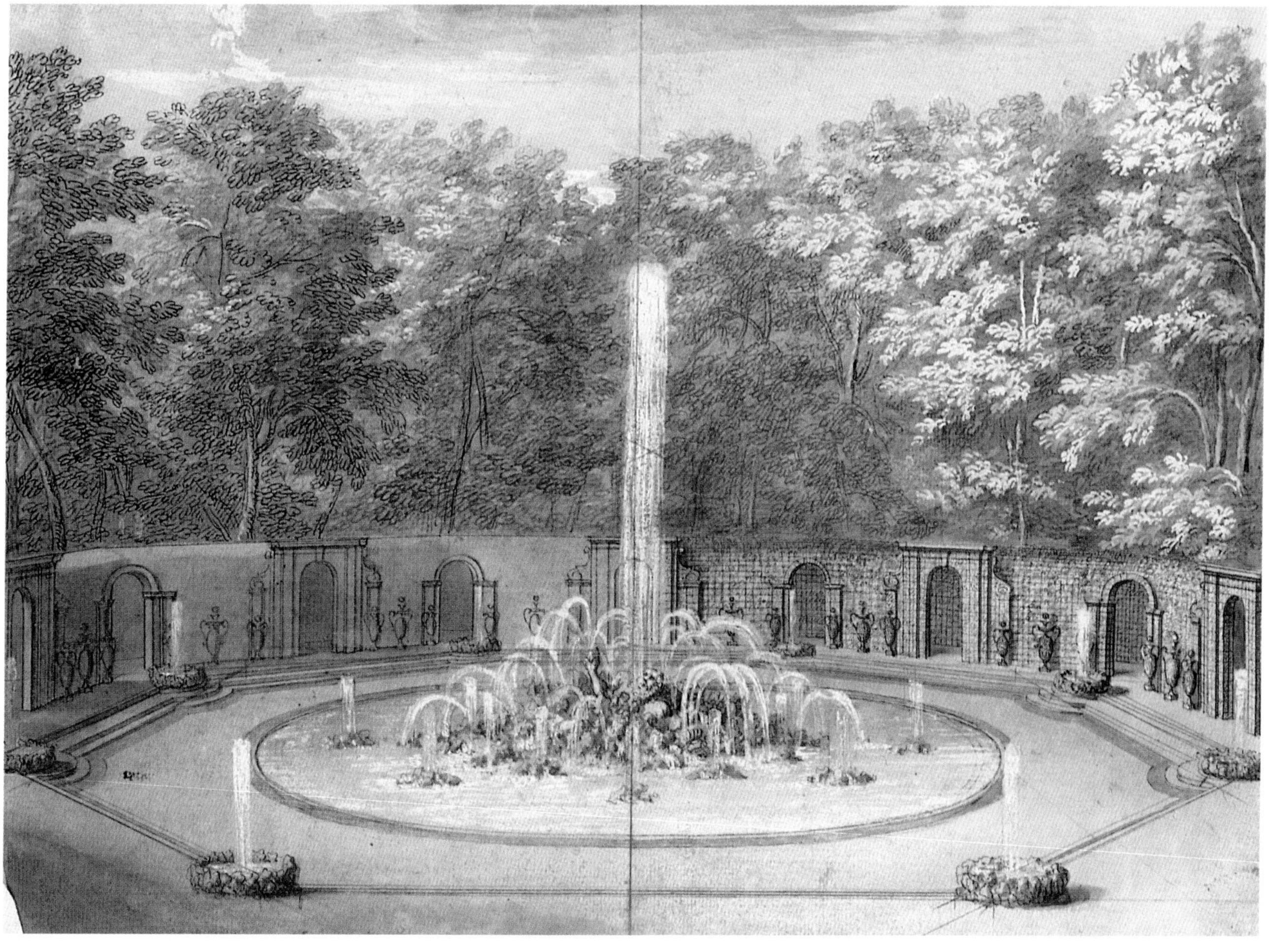

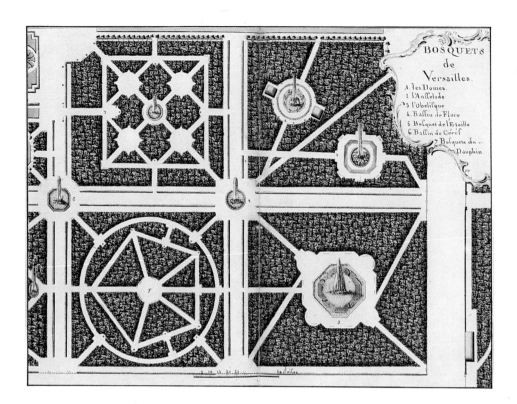

Map of the bosquets in the north-west section of the gardens of Versailles

Pierre Prieur, circa 1732

*View of Versailles*

Aveline, circa 1705

Although clumsy, this view nevertheless shows Le Nôtre's garden very clearly: the network of paths and avenues emphasized by the 'walls' of hornbeam, the rigorous cubic geometry of the vegetation which completely conceals the open-air rooms cut out of the woods and frames the extraordinary whimsical decorations.

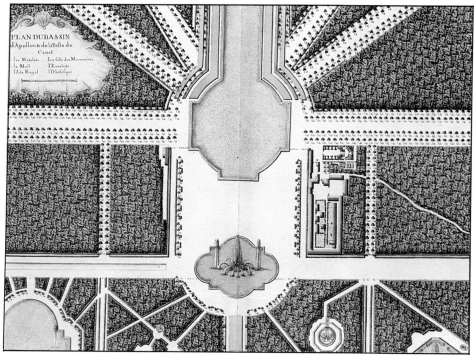

### The Bassin d'Apollon

Israël Sylvestre, seventeenth century

Until 1705, the esplanade of the pool was contained to the west by two bosquets which were wedded to the quatrefoil design, thus obscuring the view towards the Grand Canal.

### Plan of the Bassin d'Apollon and the head of the Canal

1747

In 1705, the path surrounding the Bassin d'Apollon was widened to the east by a new semi-circle and supplanted to the west by the felling of two bosquets which had obscured the view, freeing up a huge sandy esplanade lined by only two rows of trees.

*View of the head of the Grand Canal from the south side*

Circa 1710

The Versailles 'flottilla' was moored at the eastern end of the Grand Canal, next to the dockyard at Petite Venise. In the distance the semi-circular area surrounding the Bassin d'Apollon is lined with a ring of statues standing out against an avenue of alternating topiary and saplings.

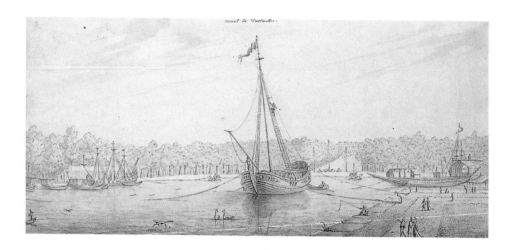

*View of the Bassin d'Apollon and the Grand Canal*

Pierre-Denis Martin, 1713

Now more or less open onto the Grand Canal, the line of the Tapis Vert was embellished with rows of majestic horse chestnuts. The ageing king was still preoccupied with his gardens, even though he could only travel around them 'on wheels'. He loved to give visitors the honour of conducting them round the gardens himself and wrote no less than six different versions of his *Manière de montrer les jardins de Versailles*.

*The Salle des Antiques*

Jean-Baptiste Martin, 1688

The Salle des Antiques, or Galerie d'Eau, was laid out to the south-east of the Bassin d'Apollon from 1680. Like a very gentle waterfall, it followed the natural slope in the ground. Water issuing from an upper fountain flowed into a double canal framing a long decorative pavement before being swallowed up by a great slope spiralling downwards.

## The Colonnade

### Jean Cotelle, 1693

Mansart's masterpiece replaced the short-lived Bosquet des Sources in 1684. Its white marble arcading seemed to cut a silhouette out of the dark foliage behind and rested on alternating columns and pillars of polychrome marble.

## Plan of the Colonnade

### Before 1699

The peristyle of 30 arcades originally had only one opening to the west. The statue depicting the Rape of Persephone, commissioned for the first Parterre d'Eau, was only placed here in 1699. Three additional entrances were created around 1704-06, reducing the number of fountains to 28.

## Jules Hardouin-Mansart (1646-1708)

### François de Troy, 1699

Mansart began to intervene in the gardens of Versailles at the end of the 1670s. From then on his ascendancy grew until some of the work by Le Brun and Le Nôtre was called into question after their respective deaths in 1690 and 1700. Little by little he erased the more whimsical, baroque creations of his predecessors, replacing them with nobler, more classical compositions.

### The Rape of Persephone

Sculpture by François Girardon, after a design by Le Brun, 1680

PLAN DE LA COLONADE.

Echelle de six Toises.
1 2 3 4 5 6

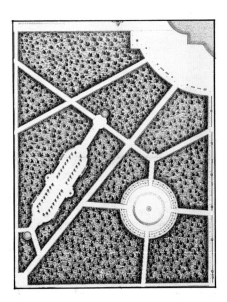

*Plan of the Salle des Marronniers
and the Colonnade*

Circa 1712

The bosquet to the south-east of
the Bassin d'Apollon appears here
in its finished state, at the end of
the reign of Louis XIV. The Salle
des Marronniers occupies the
length of the former Salle des
Antiques. The clearing in which
the Colonnade stood was opened
out by four new paths to the
points of the compass.

*The Bassin du Miroir
and the Île Royale*

Étienne Allegrain, 1688

The lake surrounding the Île
Royale began to be dug out in
1671 to the south of the gardens,
along the course of the Galie;
water from the Étang Puant was
conducted to the Bassin
d'Apollon. The lake of the Île
Royale was named after the little
rectangular island which remained
at the centre of the lake until
1684. It was completed to the east
by the Bassin du Miroir.

*The Salle de Bal*

Israël Sylvestre,
seventeenth century

### The Salle de Bal

Jean Cotelle,
commissioned in 1688

This delightful Roman amphitheatre was Le Nôtre's last work. Surrounded by graduated grass terracing, its main feature was a fan-shaped bank of cascades which tumbled over tiers of marble on its east side. These cascades were decorated with rockwork and shellwork, and completed by torchères and urns. The central arena, which was surrounded by a moat, was used as a dance-floor.

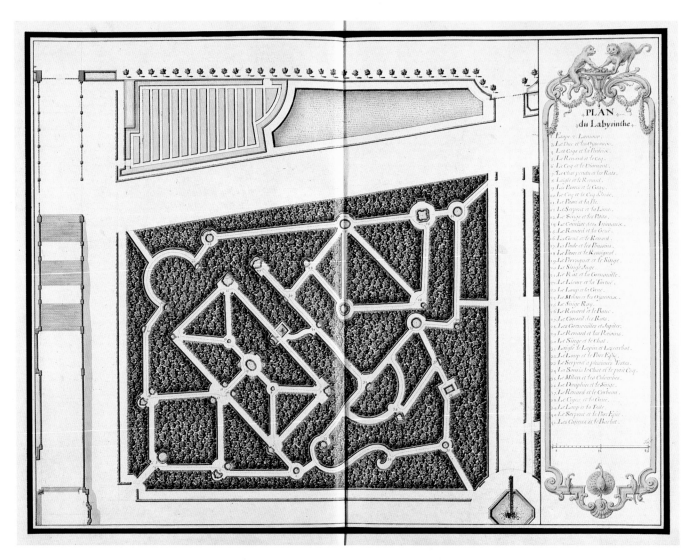

*Map of the Labyrinthe*

Jean Chaufourrier, 1720

No garden is complete without a maze. This one was devised by Charles Perrault. Le Nôtre began to lay it out in 1666. Little by little thirty-nine fountains were built into the design, based on the animals in La Fontaine's verse version of Aesop's Fables published in 1668.

*Gentlefolk promenading before the entrance of the Labyrinthe at Versailles*

Eighteenth century

*The entrance to the Labyrinthe*

Jean Cotelle, 1693

An endless variety of lead sculptures of animals, painted to look naturalistic, were featured in the fountains' trelliswork niches. The entrance to the Labyrinthe, framed by the statues of Aesop and Cupid, opened onto an overhead display of fluttering coloured birds, a kind of 'feathered ballet' illustrating the fable entitled 'The Duke and the Birds'.

In the beginning Versailles had been the retreat to which the king escaped from the court at Saint-Germain. Twenty years later it had become, by his express wish, his permanent residence. The seasons, the days and the celebration of their instigator were governed by a kind of ritual choreography codified, down to the tiniest details, by etiquette, diplomacy, the awarding of privileges and government posts, prohibitions, the laws of precedence, a formidable way of bringing pressure to bear on a nobility of whom the king was continually wary.

After a trial run at the Ménagerie, similar retreats were built for Louis at Trianon, begun in 1670, and Marly, begun after 1677. Their charms were set apart to be enjoyed by an intimate selection of the king's confidents and favourites, invited there for the day for walks or refreshments. Like extra barriers or progressive lines of retrenchment, they protected the king from the court. Access was controlled by a complex system of outer walls, gates and ditches, marking out the overlapping frontiers of their miniature territories to which one could only enter - as a royal favour - having received a letter or a word from the king.

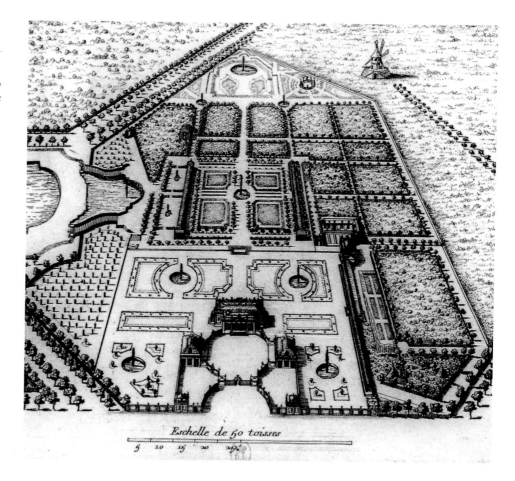

*View of Versailles,* detail of the village of Trianon

Pierre Patel, 1668

In the middle of the marshland to the north-west, the cottages of the village of Trianon cluster around the old church.

*Panoramic view to the west showing the Trianon de Porcelaine and its garden*

French School, seventeenth century

The buildings are arranged around a circular courtyard. The garden, in Le Bouteux's care, is divided into an upper parterre, next to the house, and a lower parterre, whose cross axis aligns with the branch of the Grand Canal. To the north, a long vault connects the pavilion to the Cabinet des Parfums.

In 1668 the king bought the village of Trianon and had the entire place, including its church, flattened to make way for a new château known at first as the Pavillon de Flore. Built in only a few months in 1670 as a pendant to the Ménagerie, to which it was connected via the Grand Canal, it was Le Vau's last work. In 1674 Félibien reported: 'Everybody looked upon this palace as a place of enchantment because although it was only begun at the end of the winter, it was finished by the spring, as though it had sprung up out of the ground along with the flowers in its gardens.'

The Trianon de Porcelaine, the name which stuck, was a small private house built for the use of the king and his new mistress, Madame de Montespan. Its most striking feature, according to contemporary opinion, was its delftware-covered walls inspired by a Moorish, and subsequently Spanish, technique known as *alicatado*, whereby brightly-coloured glazed pottery tiles called *azulejos* are applied to the surface of the walls. Spread throughout France by the Dutch, the delftware became confused with blue-and-white porcelain from China in the general category of 'the exotic'. The import of porcelain from the Far East was monopolized by England and the Low Countries until the creation of the Compagnie des Indes Orientales in 1664.

Under the direction of the floriculturalist Michel Le Bouteux, the garden at Trianon was dedicated to flowers in a variety and profusion never before seen at Versailles. During the summer months their scents floated through the open windows of the Appartement de Diane and the Appartement des Amours. Some 96,000 plants and two million pots buried in flowerbeds made it possible during certain seasons to change the colour and composition of the view on a daily basis, to delight the king and amaze his guests. 'All of the compartments in each of the parterres were changed, every day', wrote Saint-Simon, 'and I have seen the king and the entire court driven out of the garden, although it is vast and built in terraces overlooking the Canal, because the scent of tuberose hung so heavy in the air'.

To the north of the garden Louis XIV set up a Cabinet des Parfums for the rarest scented plants. Félibien described it as 'an extraordinarily built little palace commissioned so that several hours of the day might be whiled away here during the hot summer months'. The cultivation of orange, lemon and pomegranate trees in the open soil on a south-facing slope was an unlikely achievement. It was made possible by collapsible greenhouse frames, assembled in the autumn and taken down during the good weather. These trees also produced blossoms for the royal apartments that continued throughout the winter.

The demolition of the Trianon de Porcelaine and its replacement with the new Trianon de Marbre accompanied the fall from grace of the one for whom the former had been built and the ascension of the new favourite, Madame de Maintenon. The construction took place just as rapidly, the shell being built between June 1687 and January 1688. It joined the two main side pavilions, this time faced with stone and marble, as well as the Cabinet des Parfums, now linked to the main building by a gallery to the north of the parterres. The central part of the building was demolished, creating a space at the heart of the design framed by a majestic portico with marble columns. The effect was to create an open view of the garden which extended from the Allée de Trianon through to the Cour d'Honneur.

The garden's central ornaments, the Parterre Haut and the Parterre Bas, were only subjected to minor alterations. The main changes took place to the north, where the Jardin du Roi was created along the length of the wing

*Veüe en Perspectiue de Trianon du costé du Jardin*

*View of Trianon from the garden*

Adam Pérelle, circa 1680-84

The exterior walls are entirely covered with earthenware: Delftware on the façade, and Saint-Cloud, Lisieux, Nevers and Rouen ceramics for the roof tiles and the layers of ornament, birds and cupids crowning the roof.

*Copper vases, painted to look like porcelain, for the gardens of Trianon*

French School, seventeenth century

Painted porcelain decorations made the 'Chinese' part of the garden seem like an interior along with the wooden benches and copper vases which embellished the walks in the garden.

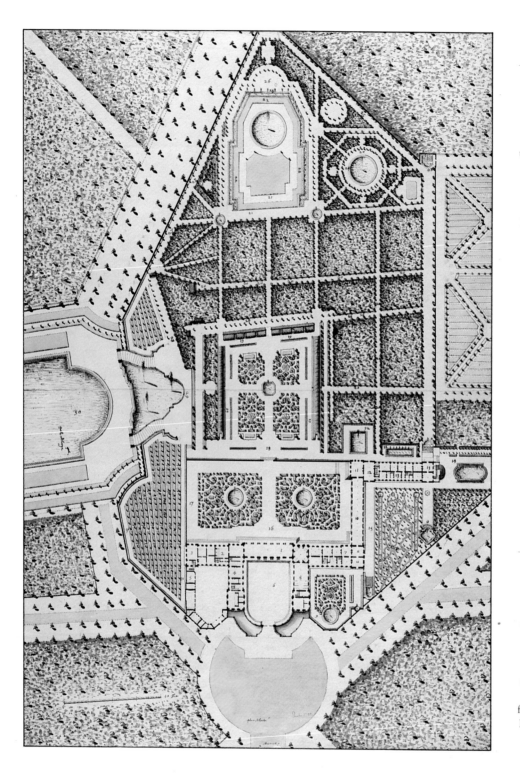

*Plan of the Trianon de Marbre
and its gardens*

Attributed to Claude Desgots,
circa 1690-1700

The construction of the Trianon
de Marbre did not prompt a
revision of the gardens, now
under Le Nôtre's supervision. The
longitudinal axis frames the
gallery of trelliswork culminating
in the Bassin du Plat-fond.
The cross axis aligns with the
Bassin du Fer-à-Cheval, extended
by the Jardin des Marronniers
in 1695. The façades of the
château open onto the private
areas known as the Jardin du Roi
and the Jardin des Sources.

*The Grand Trianon*

Jean-Baptiste Martin, 1724

Mansart and de Cotte's palace is
disposed around a courtyard
defined by two wings and a
transverse main building with an
open 'peristyle'. A long gallery
leads to the west and the former
Cabinet des Parfums, itself
extended by the wing of Trianon
sous Bois. To the north are the
flowered parterres of the Jardin du
Roi. The Bassin du Plat-fond and
the Jardin des Marronniers are
just visible in the distance.

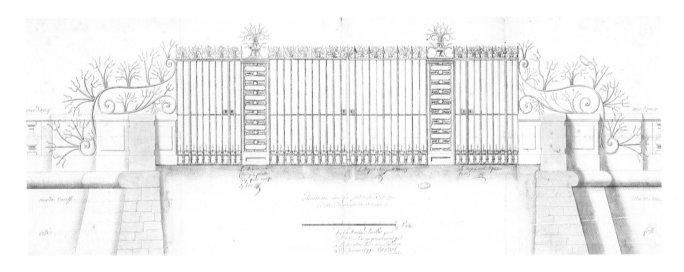

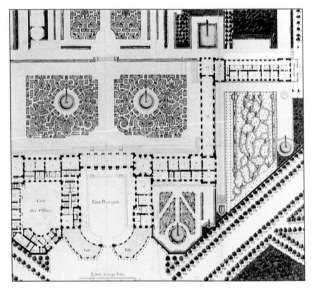

### Design for the gates of Trianon

Jules-Hardouin Mansart, 1699

The novel horizontality of the architecture of the Trianon de Marbre, devoid of projecting roofs and vertical protrusions, is reflected in the long, low line of its main gates.

### Plan of the château of Trianon and its parterres

Circa 1700

The façades open onto the different parterres created or recreated by Le Nôtre: the upper parterre with its arabesques of flowers, the box 'embroideries' garnished with flowers in the Jardin du Roi, the rocky outcrops and meandering streams of the Jardin des Sources, strewn with a random pattern of young trees. The Jardin du Roi is the only one of these gardens to have survived the alterations undertaken towards the end of the eighteenth century and during the Empire.

### The château at Trianon: view from the garden

Adam Pérelle, circa 1690

First, the general lines of a French-style garden were laid down in accordance with the scale of the site in the manner of an exercise in geometric perspective, in perfect harmony with the pure style of the façades. They served, however, simply as a basic framework which Le Nôtre was soon to cover with parterres displaying an infinite richness of motif and seasonal colour.

*The parterres and the 'peristyle' of Trianon*

Jean Cotelle, 1693

Framed by avenues of chestnut trees and galleries or screens of trelliswork covered with Spanish jasmine, the sections in the parterres are no longer made of cut-turf, but flowers: tuberose, tulips, narcissi, lilies and hyacinths are juxtaposed with wallflowers, sweet socket, pineapple weed, campanulas, valerians and carnations. These flowers were predominantly white, mauve, red and pink, and were planted in pots, facilitating swift changes of arrangement.

which looked onto the courtyard. Madame de Maintenon's apartments looked out onto this small, enclosed space, as did the king's at a later date.

The main changes took place along the gallery, right under Mansart's new classical façades, where Le Nôtre reinstated the design for his beloved Jardin des Sources, demolished several years earlier at Versailles to make way for his young rival's Colonnade. By laying out his 'barbaric' and 'chthonic' garden under the nose of Mansart's sober modernism, the old master, who was now nearly eighty, took his final revenge. The last manifesto of seventeenth-century baroque Europe's love-affair with Italy, Le Nôtre's masterpiece also points, with extraordinary foresight, to the evolution of the landscape garden. Le Nôtre himself described it lovingly, with its clever use of asymmetry, planted with trees separated by little canals 'which snake about freely and twist around trees in wide open spaces, with fountains here and there… a cool place where ladies go to work, play and have something to eat… it is the only garden I know of, apart from the Tuileries, where it is nice to walk, as well as being the loveliest. I'll leave the others, with their splendour and their grandeur'.

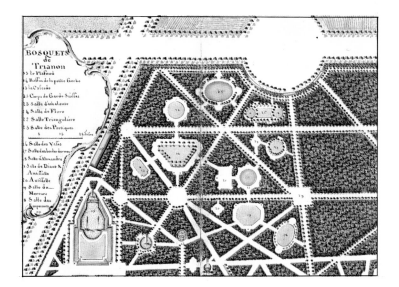

*Plan of the bosquets
at Trianon*

Pierre Prieur, 1732

After Le Nôtre's death Mansart extended the gardens towards the north-west, using the old Versailles technique of carving 'green chambers' out of the bosquets, although here complicated webs of paths and stars are inscribed within the triangular lines of woods.

*View of the château
and pavilions at Marly*

Pierre-Denis Martin, 1724

After the Trianon de Porcelaine, Louis XIV convinced himself that his estate at Marly, adjacent to the Grand Parc at Versailles, was truly the 'little hermitage' which he had been seeking. Designed by Mansart in conjunction with Le Nôtre, it quickly grew to quite a size. The château was framed by twelve pavilions dedicated to the signs of the zodiac and received only the king's favoured guests. The garden at Marly, with its 'green chambers' and its hornbeam porticoes, was the scene of constant creativity right up until the end of the reign of Louis XIV, and saw the art of topiary developed to perfection.

*A buffet d'eau or cascade
at the Trianon*

Early eighteenth century

The *buffet d'eau*, a characteristic feature in the early gardens at Versailles, was resurrected between 1700 and 1701 by Mansart in a new formation of marble and gilt-lead.

*Louis XIV (1638-1715)*

After Hyacinthe Rigaud,
eighteenth century

# The Last Days of Louis XIV

It is 1704, and the good Le Nôtre, whom the king sometimes used to honour by giving him his arm to help him get about his gardens, has been dead for four years. Dark days loom over the kingdom. In the space of less than a decade these years are going to witness most of the king's children carried away by disease.

He now knows that his own days, that procession of hours which seemed limitless when men, love and trees were young, are cruelly numbered. The work at Versailles is still continued, gardening is a long-term project, but the king's taste has changed. He has finally woken up to the fact that both his power and the nation's resources are limited.

Some of those features which had characterized the happiest years of the reign disappeared, either as a result of lassitude or thrift, in the era after Le Nôtre when the style at Versailles became less baroque and more pure and classical. Among the losses were the Bosquet du Marais, which became intolerable to Madame de Maintenon who now ruled over the ageing king, and could not bear to be reminded of the gracious muse who had been its inspiration, as well as the vaulted bowers of the Encelade and the fabulous Galerie des Antiques. However, the garden was continually being revised and embellished. The Rondeau d'Apollon, for example, now completely open to the west overlooking the Grand Canal, was modified between 1704 and 1706, and the Allée du Tapis Vert was planted with two splendid rows of horse chestnuts for the first time.

The amount of topiary work had increased throughout the garden. New walks had been planted and the hornbeam *palissades*, now fully grown, were maintained and cut back. This was the final stage in the creation of the astonishingly original green architecture of which Le Nôtre had dreamt but never really lived to see mature.

The actors themselves disappeared, one by one, Mansart in his turn in 1708, leaving the old king increasingly alone with his thoughts to contemplate their joint endeavour. How changed he was from the young Apollo, who had believed himself to be the new demi-god, master of the universe and the weather! One by one, almost unnoticed at first and then openly, the elements reclaimed their rights and the king, without a shudder and no longer taking umbrage, watched with resignation as each day they took on a firmer hold. But those closing eyes were taking with them the key to an enigma. Does the frenzy of creativity deployed at Versailles, lavished on its palace and its gardens, its successive remodellings and its enrichments over half a century, amount to anything more than momentary pleasures, the whims of a king to whom nothing could be denied, which have only survived by chance, despite the abolition of the monarchy and because of the careful work of restorers? Or was the work, on the contrary, meant to last, an accumulated legacy or mausoleum built in his lifetime in celebration of his memory, a gift to the nation and future generations?

As opposed to the buildings, which by definition in time could only fall to ruin, it was as though the garden was the great king's final remedy against death. It was the last vital gesture, a desperate and moving projection into the future which was almost as lovely as the five-year-old child, his great-grandson, the Dauphin, on whose frail shoulders rested the hopes and the responsibilities of his dynasty. Each like the other, one at the service of the other, they could not help being more beautiful tomorrow than they were today. Of that the king was sure.

*View of the Bassin de Latone*
*from the terrace*
*on the Parterre d'Eau*

Jean Rigaud, circa 1725-30

The top of the Allée du
Tapis Vert and the ramps framing
the Parterre de Latone are
bordered by rows of elongated
conifers, unclipped topiary
which has been allowed to grow
out of control.

*The Bassin d'Encelade*

Jean Rigaud, circa 1725-30

Gaspard Marsy's statue of the
giant Enceladus, with his huge jet
surrounded by a host of
complimentary frothing effects,
marks the centre of a bosquet
which has been robbed of its
trelliswork and peripheral
fountains, and where vegetation is
gradually taking over.

*The Salle des Marronniers*

Jean Rigaud, circa 1725-30

Two rows of young chestnut trees
have replaced the elaborate
decorations and fountains of the
former Salle des Antiques.
The density of the cover is due
to progressive abandoning of
pruning and pollarding, allowing
bosquets and avenues to grow into
a more 'natural' kind of garden.

*View from the Bassin de Neptune*

André-Jacques Portail, circa 1742

The trees have grown so tall that
their side branches can no longer
be cut back, resulting in branches
from trees inside the bosquets
overhanging the main paths.
Only the screens of the smaller
paths continue to be clipped into
the old walls of greenery.

# The Garden of Louis XV, the 'bien-aimé'

The garden was probably never as beautiful as it was during the Regency of Louis XV. By then it had filled out. The scarce though unmistakable remains of Louis XIII's original garden, set out nearly a century before in the middle of the thicket at Galie, invested the garden with a clear dynastic heritage which had anchored it in history. Le Nôtre and Le Brun's decisive contribution lived on, that marriage of richness and fantasy characteristic of the 1660s to the 1680s in spite of the destruction of some of the most famous bosquets. During the last two decades of the reign, on the other hand, Mansart's purifying hand had endowed it with peerless majesty and classical grandeur. But now the theatre was deserted and the actors gone; the court had fled to Paris, free at last to forget itself in business and pleasure. The great vessel, although abandoned by its passengers, sailed on. The gardeners tended the flowers in the parterres, the pruners dragged their enormous ladders on wheels across the walks and exhausted themselves using their garden tools, the fountain engineers still celebrated the ritual of the water shows, and the kitchen garden continued to produce miracles from its glasshouses and espaliers, but all in vain. The immutable machine, perfectly regulated by decades of functioning with the sole aim of glorifying its creator and master, now seemed to be running in neutral. Its pointlessness only increased with the addition of each new layer, like extra souls perhaps already tainted by nostalgia.

Until at last, during a spring day in the 1720s, the first leaf, whether it was from a hornbeam, an elm or a lime — either unconsciously or on purpose, — which dared to escape from the *palissade*, cleared the string boundary, and crossing the intangible order of the green geometry, finished off the masterpiece with a new and subtle touch of poetry. The spirit of this more relaxed garden, softened by allowing the hornbeam walks to grow more naturally, was captured in Jacques Rigaud's ravishing series of engravings carried out between 1725 and 1730.

Louis XV, nicknamed '*bien-aimé*' or 'well-beloved' by his people, came to live at Versailles on 15 June 1722. It seemed that he had neither the taste, nor the desire, nor the means to take up the enormous operation masterminded by his great-grandfather, but he certainly could not ignore its symbolic aura, the basis of his own power. The new king's contribution to the gardens at Versailles was merely to continue to run it and to add the final touches. The only significant alterations were the filling-in of the Étang de Clagny, which had become unhealthy, and the completion of the Bassin de Neptune with a series of fantastic allegories and marine monsters carried out between 1738 and 1741 by the sculptors Adam, Lemoine and Bouchardon. With these exceptions, Louis XV more or less contented himself with rearranging space in the palace and the park so that it was better suited to his own pleasurable way of life. Meanwhile, it was up to Nature, through the remarkable act of growth, to take on the role of transforming the garden by herself.

Very gradually, geometry, which until now had governed the green architecture, gently began to loosen its grip. Negligence, lack of interest and reduced means along with the new taste for more natural, more spontaneous scenery like the settings in paintings by Watteau, Oudry or Boucher were the precursors of a new mood which led to the progressive abandoning of the clipped vaults, the screens and the *palissades*. They had become ever more perilous to reach with each passing year as gardeners balanced on top of unstable scaffolding, harder to attend to as the weight of the branches, thicker with every season, made them increasingly unyielding to garden tools. Free at last, the trees at the heart of the bosquets, now nearly a hundred years old, had grown, unfettered, to 30 or 40 metres high. Seeking the light, their top branches,

*View of the château
and the orangery from
the Pièce d'eau des Suisses*

André-Jacques Portail, circa 1741

The façade of the orangery faces
the sun and the rows of orange
trees lined up in their boxes.
To the west the trees have already
grown to double the height of the
palissades. In the background
statues stand in niches cut out
of the façade of the bosquets.

*The Yew Ball, 25 February 1748*

Charles-Nicolas Cochin the Elder,
eighteenth century

Topiary remained one of the chief
characteristics of the French
garden. Enthusiasm for the art
sometimes reached the heights
of absurdity and was the pretext
for the extravagant costumes worn
at this masked ball.

*The Bassin de Neptune*

André-Jacques Portail, circa 1740

This view of the Bassin de
Neptune, complete with its lead
decorations, provides invaluable
information about the state of the
vegetation at the time: geometric
shapes are maintained, the screens
along the smaller paths remain,
the trees inside the bosquets
have grown, their side branches
resting on the low hornbeam
hedges. Topiary alternates
with fountains at the beginning
of the Allée d'Eau.

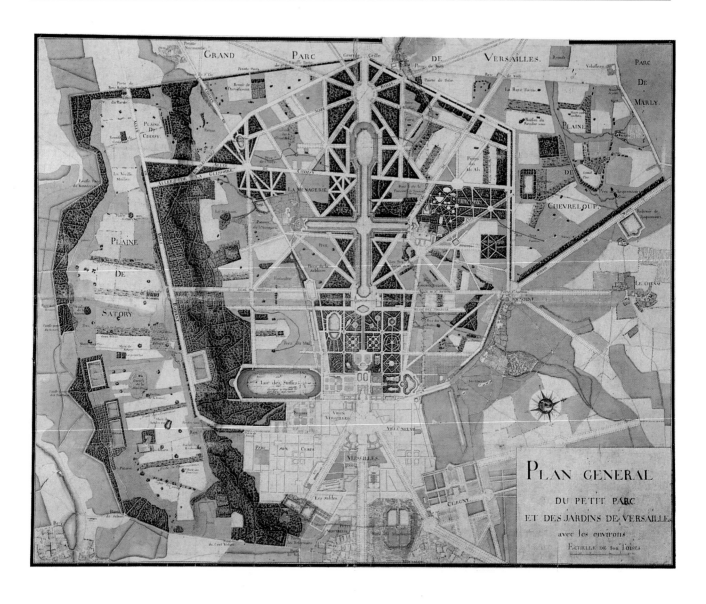

formerly ruthlessly cut back, had grown too tall to be pollarded and were now completely beyond control. Spreading out above the walks, they covered the sides of the *palissades*, whose vertical pruning continued right up to the top, which the pruners reached by climbing onto the heavy, lower branches of fallen foliage, creating the cut *en marquise*, so characteristic of Versailles during the second half of the eighteenth century.

The king's appetite for pleasure found a more natural expression in the intimate and comfortable surroundings of Trianon than at Versailles. The palace at Trianon was, in a sense, the perfect retreat and his latest favourite, Madame de Pompadour, persuaded him to build a new Ménagerie here. Thus he revived the tradition taken up by Louis XIV at the far end of the southern branch of the Canal. But this new Ménagerie was completely novel: instead

*Map of the Petit Parc and the Versailles gardens, the 'Boileau map'*

Boileau, 1744

Versailles is seen at its apogee, complete with all its annexed estates: the Ménagerie, Trianon, Marly and Clagny, the plains of Satory and Chèvreloup and the Grand Parc: a constellation arranged around the different palaces and their respective gardens, a complex patchwork of woods and fields, punctuated with numerous reservoirs and nurseries, woven together by a network of paths and avenues.

*Louis XV (1710-74)*

Maurice Quentin de la Tour

*Madame de Pompadour (1721-64)*

Carle Van Loo

of trying to acclimatize wild animals or beasts from exotic climes, it housed ordinary domestic breeds, cows from Holland, sheep, pigeons and rare poultry species used for cross-breeding. This project showed a noticeable change in attitude towards nature, through a kind of idealization of rural life contemporary with the popularization of classical pastoral scenes in the decorative arts, and a pre-romantic vision of the universe which developed in parallel with the publication of Jean-Jacques Rousseau's first writings in 1750. It also reflects the emergence of the new thinking of the *encyclopédistes,* that encompassed a desire to catalogue and classify all living things and all human knowledge. It also witnessed the direct influence of François Quesnay, the Marquise de Pompadour's doctor, on the king. Quesnay founded the physiocrat school, an intellectual movement which believed that land was the only source of wealth and improved produce and modes of agricultural production to be the driving force behind a global reorganization of society.

The Nouvelle Ménagerie, dominated by the dairy, was built to the north-east of the Trianon palace. It included a garden, part of which was reserved at first for produce but which was later given over entirely to ornamental plants. It was designed, as were the various other buildings, by the architect Ange-Jacques Gabriel. The garden's overall composition conformed to the French formula in that its development was graduated, and a series of symmetrical parts issued from a hierarchy of criss-crossing axes. It was a rare example of the continuation into the second half of the eighteenth century of a type of garden design which disappeared barely ten years later in the face of a sudden craze for a new kind of garden imported from England. But it cannot be regarded as a backward-looking work. It testifies to the contrary because after Le Nôtre, whose signed drawings are still extremely rare, had supplied the idea of laying out a garden with planting lines and stakes, a method only recorded *a posteriori* by Dezallier d'Argenville in his *Théorie et pratique du jardinage*, a number of masters, architects in particular, dedicated themselves over the next half century to perfecting the formula deployed to such spectacular effect at Versailles. Only this time they did it with graphite at the drawing-board. Gabriel fell into this category. However, he did possess his own style of gardening, illustrated by the different examples he created at Choisy, at the small palace at Fontainebleau, at Compiègne, and here at Trianon.

Most of the features of his style are here: the cross-shaped composition, the long, low parterres, the huge central esplanade sunk with basins and bordered by rows of trees, framed by narrow, low bosquets with little green glades cut out of them, like green rooms overhung by quincunxes of trees, the taste for circular and oval shapes, in the form of pools, parterres, glades or clipped box with palmette motifs.

The king's architect-in-chief proved his inventiveness with an original design for two great circular cross walks, which stimulated a constant feeling of discovery in the visitor, but especially with the delightful Labyrinthe, punctuated by open-air salons conducive to amorous meetings, which wove its circuitous way through the western fringes of the garden. The Labyrinthe resurrected Charles Perrault's precedent, whilst also heralding the serpentine meanderings of the walks in the future Jardin anglais, through the introduction of asymmetry within symmetry.

A surprising revival of the art of pruning was not the least of his innovations. Gabriel's garden at Trianon effectively maintained the tradition of strictly pruned gardens, the expressions of extreme interventionism which, although they had endured at Versailles for nearly a century, had ultimately become uncontrollable and thus proved their limitations. Without losing a single one of the features which characterized the French style, pools, parterres, bosquets and straight avenues of trees, Gabriel on the other hand took shrewd note of

*View of the Trianon gardens, with the Ménagerie and the Pavillon Français*

Attributed to André-Jacques Portail, circa 1751

To mark the crossing of the two axes which anchored the composition accompanying the new Ménagerie (to the left), Gabriel added the present Pavillon français between 1749 and 1750. An elegant kiosk used as a little salon where a small group might go to play a game of cards, it was set in an ornamental garden with low bosquets, green glades, pools, avenues and parterres.

*Trelliswork portico at the Nouvelle Ménagerie kitchen garden*

Circa 1750

To the east, beyond the Pavillon français, were the hen-houses, which divided the chickens into 'fine fowl' and 'common fowl', the fig house, the aviaries, the hot-beds and the conservatories, followed by the vegetable gardens, which stopped at a trelliswork portico marking the end of the garden's longitudinal axis.

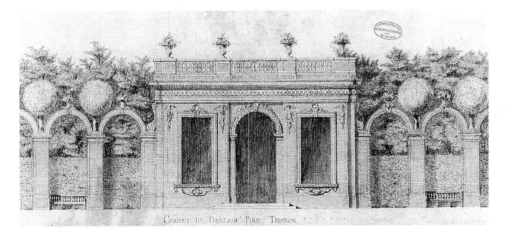

CABINET DE TREILLAGE POUR TRIANON

*The cool room in the garden at the Nouvelle Ménagerie*

Attributed to Langelin, circa 1753

The cross axis ended up at a second pavilion, built between 1751 and 1753, which served as a little dining-room for sampling produce from the dairy and the vegetable garden. On each side were two arcaded trelliswork galleries with pillars incorporating elongated trees crowned by topiary balls.

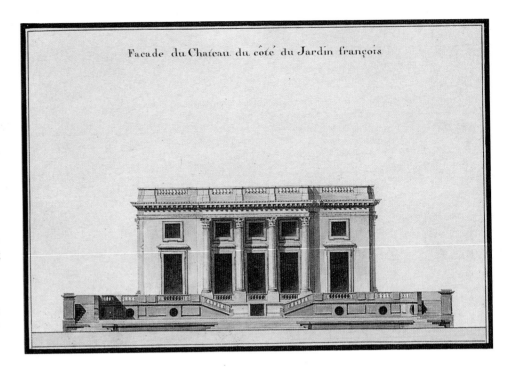

Façade du Chateau du côté du Jardin françois

*Façade of the Petit Trianon
viewed from the Jardin français*

Claude-Louis Châtelet, 1786

The construction of Gabriel's masterpiece, the Petit Trianon, between 1762 and 1766, resulted in the total destruction of the vegetable garden at the end of the main axis. To create a more fitting setting for the new façade, a veritable neo-classical manifesto, the ornamental gardens between the Pavillon français and the Petit Trianon were extended, bosquets and parterres replacing vegetable gardens and aviaries.

Louis XIV's technical and horticultural failures at Versailles and radically reduced the scale of both the buildings and the garden at the new Trianon. Whereas the gardens at Versailles covered more than 225 acres, the new Petit Trianon's took up scarcely five. The tops of the hedges were fixed at the low height of about seven metres, the bosquets covered less than 15 acres. The space between the trees was reduced to about three metres, the limit of what was reasonable to preserve the generosity and monumentality of the long vistas in spite of the overall reduction in the scale of the whole project. Thus Gabriel developed a skilful work in miniature, which relied on a cunning artifice of scale, whilst at the same time responded to financial constraints, the desire for intimacy, and the need to make garden maintenance more practical. This new approach to scale and form was not dissimilar to the early descriptions and pictures of a type of exotic miniature landscape where everything conspired to make the garden look bigger.

The west façade of the Petit Trianon was now aligned with the symmetrical perspectives of the Jardin de la Nouvelle Ménagerie (not actually known by its present name, the Jardin français until 1774, as opposed to the new Jardin anglais). However, the windows of its north and east façades, with their noble aspects marked by Greece and Antiquity, looked onto a tiny and unusual compartmentalized garden. From 1761 this land was actually set aside for

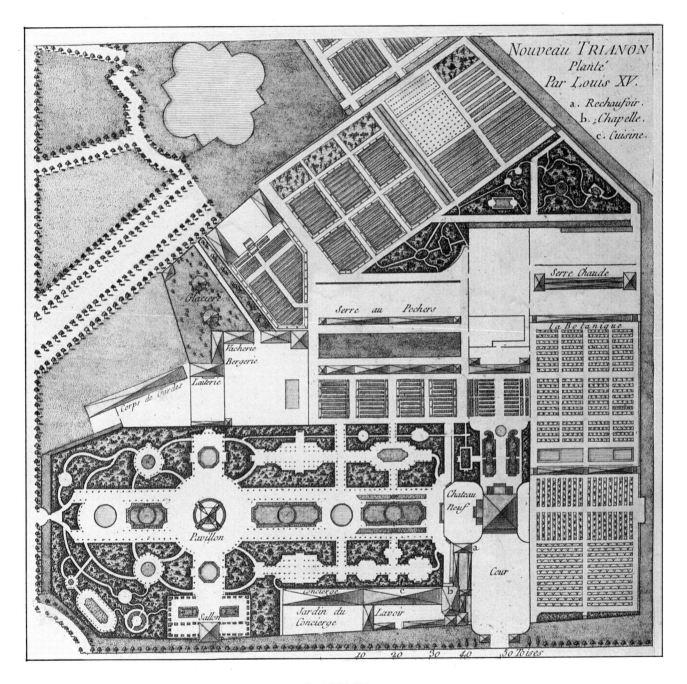

*Louis XV's Trianon*

Georges-Louis Le Rouge, 1774

The construction of the new palace precipitated the addition of a succession of new gardens. Each of its four façades opened onto a different view, the courtyard, the ornamental garden, the small parterre - which ended up at the greenhouses, and finally, the Botanical Garden.

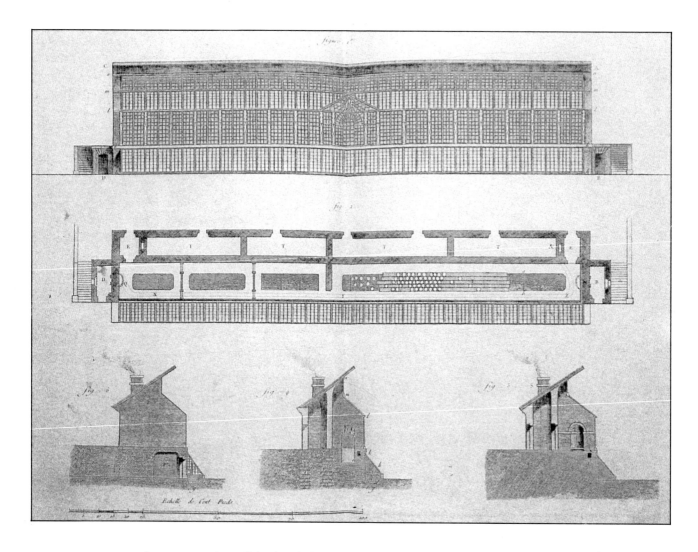

the conservation of the king's botanical collection, displayed on boards arranged in squares according to Bernard de Jussieu's scientific classification. The king, who was passionate about botanical research, found it a soothing distraction from affairs of state.

Maintained by the gardener Claude Richard, the botanical collection was enriched with rare varieties which his son, Antoine, brought back from his many foreign trips, gradually enlarged, and equipped with a number of greenhouses including a large, heated 'Dutch greenhouse', used for cultivating tropical vegetables. With up to four thousand varieties, the botanical garden at Trianon was one of the most famous and celebrated in Europe. Its destruction, less than fourteen years after it had been built, was one of the most irreparable losses in the history of the gardens at Versailles.

*Refreshment tents erected in the gardens of the Petit Trianon*

Second half of
the eighteenth century

*The large greenhouse
at the Petit Trianon*

Plate from the *Grande
Encyclopédie*, 1762

This extraordinary structure was
built by Louis XV in imitation of
the latest 'Dutch greenhouse'.
It combined projecting south-east
facing panes of glass with thermal,
warmth-absorbing masonry walls,
reinforced by heating which
permitted the cultivation of
numerous varieties of exotic plants.

*View of the château of Versailles
from the Pièce d'eau des Suisses*

Nicolas-Marie Ozanne, 1764

*The Bosquet des Bains d'Apollon during the felling which took place during the winters of 1774-75*

Hubert Robert, 1775-77

Various forestry procedures including towing, felling, measuring logs, cutting and uprooting stumps, are carried out in front of the statues of the Parterre du Nord and one of the sculptures from the Bains d'Apollon, dominated by the silhouettes of the ancient conifers framing ramps of the Parterre de Latone.

# The Replanting of Versailles

The magnificent *fêtes* held at Versailles in honour of the marriage of the Dauphin's son, the future Louis XVI, to the young Archduchess Marie-Antoinette of Austria, were the last seen during the reign of Louis XV who was to die four years later.

For a last time the boughs of the old trees planted by Louis XIV were lit up for a single evening. These venerable ancestors, some of them more than a hundred years old, had long borne the pathetic scars of the treatment they had suffered in their youth, when they were brutally torn up from their primitive forests, afflicted by the long journey in howling winds and planted too closely only to be martyred by coppicing and pruning. In spite of partial replanting of more than 8,000 trees, undertaken in 1747 in an attempt to check the devastation caused by exceptionally cruel frosts during the winters of 1709 and 1730, and devastating storms in April 1740, the damage was irreparable. Nothing more could be done. The trees had to be chopped down.

Louis XV was not a man of decision. If he finally gave in to constant pressure from Gabriel, who had long ago set his sights on launching the *grand projet*, the complete renovation of the old brick and stone town façade, he hesitated and procrastinated over the violation of Louis XIV's gardens and bringing down the axe on the bosquets. He arrived at the end of his own life, on the 10 May 1774, having deferred this cruel sentence.

It was therefore up to his successor, Louis XVI, to tackle this painful task with courage after his accession to the throne. It took two winters, between December 1774 and March 1776, to cut down the ancient plantations, the majestic forest cathedral. The Comte d'Angiviller, a friend of the king's who had been recently promoted to the department of architecture, with his assistant Cuvillier, had special responsibility for the replanting scheme. In order to achieve their aim, Angiviller and Cuvillier sought the advice of the greatest authorities of the time, the Abbé Nolin, controller of the king's nurseries, and the gardeners Thouin and Lemoine.

While the bosquets rang with the sound of the woodman's axe and caved in like palaces of cards, the inevitable and difficult debate about the appearance of the new plantations began. Should one, in anticipation of the garden's future historical importance to the nation, fully replace what others would no

*The great lighting display in the park, held in honour of the marriage of the Dauphin to the Archduchess Marie-Antoinette, on 19 May 1770*

Jean-Michel Moreau the Younger, 1770

This view was taken from the bottom of the Tapis Vert, in the direction of the Bassin d'Apollon and the Grand Canal.

*The Allée de la Dormeuse*

Hubert Robert, circa 1773

The unchecked growth and the decrepitude of the trees progressively undermined the original symmetry established between the stone walls of the orangery and the vegetal walls of the *palissades* and bosquets.

*Louis XVI (1754-93)*

Joseph-Siffrède Duplessis, 1775

longer hesitate to condemn as the 'boring' rigour of design in the French tradition? Was it not time, instead, to abandon what had become out-dated in favour of the new English style, which was much more fashionable and representative of the latest ideas flourishing in the second half of the Age of Enlightenment? Which varieties should be planted? Should they be the kind traditionally found in classical French woods, or should one opt for the highly-prized new exotic species being imported by merchant ships from the four corners of the globe?

The debate assumed a symbolic, and by extention, political dimension. How could this calling into question of the gardens at Versailles avoid being perceived as the first challenge to the powers that had created it? Could Le Nôtre be criticized and Louis XIV spared, could the work of art be written off without violating the memory of the patron, the rules of the symmetrical garden be contested without being seen to attack the principle of divine right of kings, the splendour of which it expressed so brilliantly? And finally, could the garden even be discussed without bringing the authority of the monarchy into the debate?

Louis XVI could not have been unaware of the thorny stakes in this battle which his councillors and courtiers waged around him and into which he had been so brutally plunged. To any other landowner it would have been no more than an ordinary forestry problem. The catastrophic state of the kingdom's

### The Entrance to the Tapis Vert

#### Hubert Robert, 1775-77

This painting shows the king and queen visiting the sawmill in the park. The felling of the Bosquet de la Girandole and the screens of the avenues has opened up strange, deep views of the Colonnade, the Grand Canal and the pavilions of the Bosquet des Dômes. The gloomy skeletons of great trees stand out against a winter sky, next to the last remaining conifers which mark the entrance to the Tapis Vert.

economy on the death of his predecessor provided the king with the most convincing argument for bringing these inconclusive discussions to an end.

If the economics of the replanting exercise cannot be considered the sole factor in determining which trees were felled and which replanted, we must recognize that it played a far from negligible role. The areas to be felled were first assessed by Courtois, the 'wood merchant', and they returned a revenue of 150,000 *livres* to the coffers of the Bâtiments du Roi in May 1776, paying for a large part of the restoration costs. The subsequent replanting of an identical scheme, which did not disrupt either the line of the avenues or the positioning of statues and fountains, would considerably minimize the cost of building terraces and other works, managed by a pair of businessmen, Jules Crosner and Louis Berte.

Finally, the abandoning of a general demand for expensive foreign species, though warmly recommended by Thouin and Nolin, was a considerable saving. In fact home-grown trees were readily available, plantings having been made originally to satisfy the needs of the navy. Local nurseries supplied, at low prices, 6,000 oak saplings, about 2,500 poplars, 2,000 maples and 2,000 silver-birch and hornbeams to replant the bosquets. In conclusion, if the general lines of Le Nôtre's design were not universally called into question, certain definite modifications were made. One, which was fundamental, was the replacement of kilometre upon kilometre of austere green walls of hornbeam, *palissades* and screens with graceful and transparent colonnades of single young chestnuts and limes, planted in straight rows. The designs for the replanting, submitted to Angiviller by Michel Hazon, the Intendant des Bâtiments, in October 1775, accentuated the open vistas in a garden which was now increasingly accessible to the public, by multiplying the number of diagonal walks. This allowed the fountains to be approached from new directions.

Simultaneously, the Dauphin and the Girandole, the two oldest bosquets at

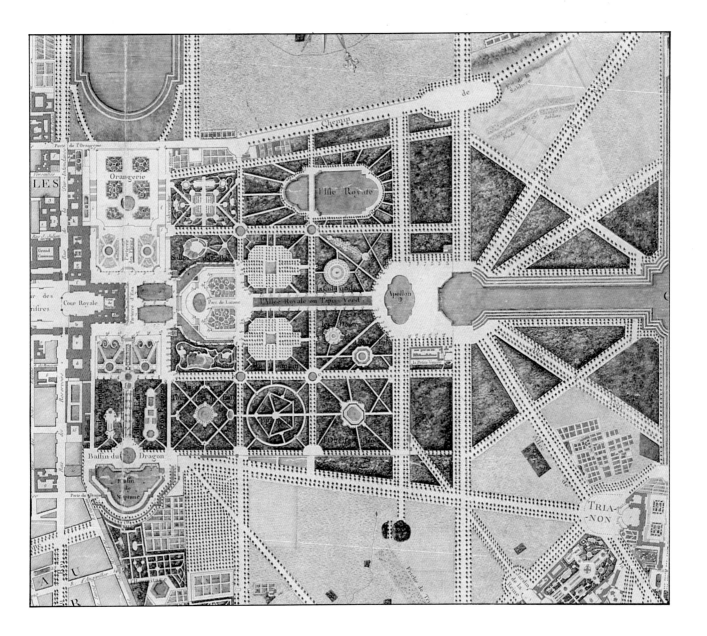

*Design for the Bains d'Apollon*

Hubert Robert, circa 1775

Versailles, were destroyed to make way for two new symmetrical quincunxes, the North Quincunx and the South Quincunx scooped out inside to provide the stroller with the pleasure and shade of alternating limes and chestnuts. Old Louis XIV designs were relentlessly massacred when the last traces of the Théâtre d'Eau were erased. This along with the closure and subsequent abandonment of the dilapidated Arc de Triomphe, for reasons of economy, left space for the new Rond Vert. While symmetry in the traditional French style predominated in the public parts of the garden, there were two private bosquets, enclosed by railings, where the sovereigns themselves could experiment with more innovative styles.

The first was the Labyrinthe with its naturalistically painted lead bestiary. This had become really old-fashioned and seriously damaged by fallen branches and was sacrificed to the Bosquet de la Reine, the Queen's Grove. Its new composition, punctuated with tiny green *salons* surrounded by valuable trees such as Corsican pine, cedar of Lebanon and tulip trees from Virginia, was belted by a network of walks, *en tortillets*, a modern version of the old maze. This bosquet became famous for being the scene of one of the murkier episodes in the unfortunate 'Story of the diamond necklace' immortalized in the novel by Alexandre Dumas. The other was the Bosquet des Bains d'Apollon. Hazon's first design for this, still perfectly symmetrical, was rejected. Richard Mique, the queen's new architect, was also consulted. But the commission finally went to the painter Hubert Robert (assisted by the architect Heurtier) who submitted a drawing which the king judged to be 'good', on 17 February 1778. Three groups of marble statuary were exhibited here in their fourth different place. They were originally designed for the first Grotte de Thétis but transferred to the Bosquet des Dômes in 1684, only to be taken away to the old Marais in 1704. This time round they were displayed in a setting which perfectly expressed the new Picturesque taste, in deliberate contrast to the aesthetic adopted elsewhere in the garden. Their positioning, at the entrance to a mysterious grotto at the bottom of a shady, secret wood, set off their immaculate whiteness to brilliant effect. The grotto was the new Bains d'Apollon finished in 1780. It had a rustic colonnade framed by cascades which opened onto the side of an artificial mountain crowned with fir trees. It was one of the Ancien Régime's most misunderstood but most magical designs, and added the finishing touch to the garden.

*The Grand Trianon from the*
*north branch of the Grand Canal*

Louis-Nicolas de Lespinasse, 1780

RECEUIL
des Plans du Petit
Trianon

Par le Sʳ Mique Chevalier
de L'ordre de Sᵗ Michel
Premier Architecte
honoraire Intendant
General des Batimens
du Roy et de la
Reine.
1786.

*Frontispiece from* Recueil
des Plans du Petit Trianon

Claude-Louis Châtelet and
Richard Mique, 1786

When Archduke Ferdinand,
governor of Lombardy and brother
of the queen, visited Versailles and
Trianon in 1786, he was presented
with a souvenir album which gives
an invaluable description of the
Petit Trianon's buildings and
gardens. It is now housed at the
Biblioteca Estense in Modena.

# Trianon and the Jardin anglais

I f Louis XVI made only minor concessions to the sirens who tempted him to redesign Le Nôtre's gardens at Versailles, the situation at Trianon was very different.

In 1774 he gave his young wife the enchanting pavilion and its little gardens which Ange-Jacques Gabriel had designed for Louis XV and Madame de Pompadour. Far from the fastidious grandeur of the court, far from the complex protocol and the prying eyes of the crowds, the queen created a sheltered world where she could behave and do as she liked without being constantly subjected to scrutiny. Here she could surround herself with her own friends and escape from the impositions of court officials, free herself from the pompous setting inherited from the previous century and create her own fresher and more youthful environment.

She moved in at once, choosing a north-facing apartment on the first floor at the onset of summer. At first she only came here from time to time, perhaps for an afternoon excursion, Versailles was only a quarter of a league away, but she soon developed the habit of lunching at Trianon and passing three or four hours here with a small group of close friends and companions. The king often joined her towards the end of the afternoon for conversation or a game of cards.

However, she did not spend the night here until the spring of 1779, when an attack of measles determined that she should be separated from the king for a three-week convalescence. Nevertheless, there were few complaints when the separation was extended. After this she visited much more frequently, creating an inner circle among whom shone her great friends, the Princesse de Lamballe, the Comtesse de Polignac and the Comte d'Artois, the king's younger brother. As a result of the closed nature of this little coterie to which even the queen's ladies-in-waiting were not admitted by right, certain unwise decisions were taken. For example, a draconian notice forbidding the public to enter, 'By order of the queen', was attached to the gates of the queen's private residence, quickly provoking jealousy and gossip. The nickname 'Little Vienna', originally invented out of sympathy for the young archduchess, now had more critical connotations. The secrecy which cloaked the forbidden 'pleasures of Trianon' could not fail to excite all sorts of speculation about their nature and their intensity, and stirred up rancour and calumny among the queen's detractors who, naturally, were not invited to share them. With hindsight these activities look trivial and charming, almost childish, sometimes ridiculous to the point of irresponsibility. They certainly did nothing to strengthen the image of a king now practically dismissed by his wife whom some people said was surrounded by suitors.

Gambling was the chief of these 'pleasures', and it went on heavily at Trianon. Everyone got together round the tables during the afternoon or after supper. Winnings and losses at trictrac, whist or lotto could mount up to thousands of *livres*. Joseph II, the Emperor of Austria, and the queen's brother, grew anxious for his sister's reputation, as he was informed of these extravagant faro parties, described as 'boisterous and indecent', where the ladies of the Court were sometimes caught playing 'carelessly', as it was euphemistically put.

The theatre also enjoyed the queen's patronage. At the time the licentiousness, atheism and even subversiveness of plays, which were presumed to reflect the moral standards of the actors themselves, meant that the art was still sullied by a reputation which the Church and moral standards condemned to the point where they were performed almost clandestinely in aristocratic households. In 1775 the first *Salle* was set up in the gallery at the Grand Trianon. It was a canvas-covered wooden frame with boards. The following year it was taken down and set up in the orangery at the Petit Trianon, but the temporary theatre was rather limiting because it lacked arches and space underneath in which to put the machinery which changed the scenes. So Marie-Antoinette asked Richard Mique, who had recently been appointed to the task of supervising building work at Trianon, to come up with a new theatre with modern technical inventions, based on the theatre at Choisy.

Mique's theatre was built to the north of the Jardin français, between the hornbeam bosquets and the large greenhouse. It was linked to the Petit Trianon by the Corridor de la Comédie, a gallery with young wood porticoes, covered with greyish-brown cloth in good weather as a protection against the heat of the sun. On evenings when there were performances, dozens of little oil lamps glimmered among the branches of the hornbeams along the walks. There was a twin exit gallery to the south, flanked by the chapel Louis XV had built, whose bulbous bell-tower supported the cross of the Redeemer, and the new temple to the arts with the sculpture of a child and a lyre, *The Genius*

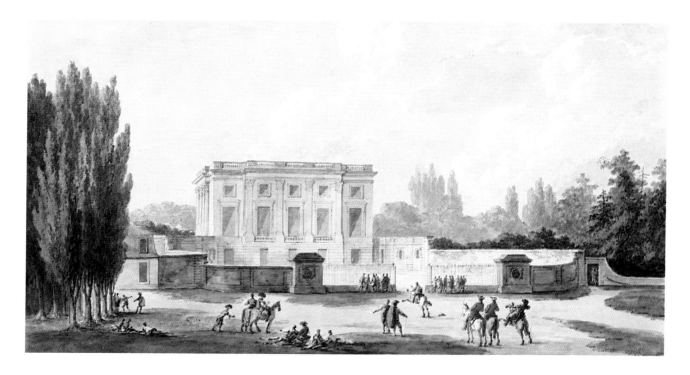

*The Petit Trianon
from the courtyard*

Claude-Louis Châtelet, 1786

*of Apollo*, on the façade flanked by the two grimacing masks of Tragedy and Comedy. In this way the queen and her residence were incorporated into the general symbolism.

The queen devoted herself enthusiastically to court theatricals in her new theatre. Spectators acted opposite professional singers and actors in a range of operas, comic operas and plays. Michel-Jean Sedaine and Charles-Simon Favart wrote the librettos for *Aucassin et Nicolette, Le Roi et le Fermier, La Gageure imprévue* and *Isabelle et Gertrude*. On 19 September 1780, the queen — who was particularly fond of playing amorous shepherdesses and innocent maidservants — worked wonders with the role of the lovely Colette in a production of Jean-Jacques Rousseau's *Devin du Village*, which she sang in a 'very pleasant and tuneful voice'. Most of the plays were light and rustic. They told the stories of the ephemeral love affairs of peasants, so dear to the late-eighteenth century, indulging the fashionable obsession with the lives and customs of country folk which led directly to playing at 'farming' at the Hameau, the hamlet built especially for Marie-Antoinette.

The most innocent of all the delights at Trianon was definitely the garden. However, that is not to imply that it was anything short of exquisite and lavish. It only took several years for the new Jardin anglais to capture the imaginations of the most enlightened members of the aristocratic elite. Most of them adopted the new style with a frenzy which had hazardous results and often devoured their fortunes.

At court, in the salons and country houses, people spoke of nothing else, did nothing else. They trafficked in plants from Oregon, bullied village carpenters into making chinoiserie, competed, paying astronomic prices, for one or other of the gardeners from across the Channel, believed to be a virtuoso in possession of the secrets of the latest techniques, often only to be disappointed with the results.

There are many explanations for the craze. The first was that it was a reaction to the 'French style', of which the garden at Versailles was the undisputed archetype. However, this style was already perceived, somewhat unjustly, through the double distorting lens of the somewhat austere nature of the simplifications brought about towards the end of Louis XIV's reign, and the 'ordinarinesss' of the gardens then produced — typified by Mariette's unremarkable engravings — which bore little comparison to the burgeoning inventiveness of the early layouts. The same stereotyped gardens were reproduced over and over again, a series of never-ending clichés. Even Nature herself grew weary of these ageing compositions. It all seemed so sad, so outdated, and no longer impressed anybody except the bourgeoisie and provincial squires.

At the opposite extreme, the English garden seemed to epitomize every virtue. The eighteenth-century was the age of discovery, of exploration and exoticism, initiated on the other side of the Channel. Travellers, scholarly dilettantes and artists, were returning from abroad full of amazing stories, laden with sketches for gardens which looked as though they had come straight from the hand of the Creator. Composed of swathes of untouched nature or rustic landscapes, strewn with little follies, obelisks, grottoes and rotundas, they were conducive to poetic feelings and philosophical reflection. Their lines were fluid and sweeping, and totally lacking in symmetry. Vegetation was free to grow into its own forms, safe from the pruner's shears. But the irregularity, the obsession with banishing planting strings and levels, the interlacing and circuitousness, were not really new as Le Nôtre had already demonstrated at Versailles.

From 1700 the English had made it possible to carry out designs on a considerably enlarged scale thanks to the general adoption of the enclosure system.

*The Jardin français
at the Petit Trianon*

Louis-Nicolas de Lespinasse,
circa 1780

The former garden of the
Nouvelle Ménagerie, designed
by Gabriel for Louis XV, had
finally reached full maturity
30 years after it had been planted.
Even though it was now
unfashionable, it was maintained.
Its immaculate vaults continued
to be clipped in keeping with the
French style because it provided a
necesssary contrast with the new
Jardin anglais next door.

By appropriating and cultivating fallow land, it assured the resurrection of under-exploited great estates ravaged by half a century of civil war, and permitted the renovation of agriculture and forestry. Freed from land constraints, English gardening now took in the whole countryside, creating a range of effects which reflected all the different nuances between Chaos and the Garden of Eden, depending on which estate and during which part of the eighteenth century they were produced.

The style was clearly composed of a mixture of different influences synthesized in England. The first came from China, the paradigm of exoticism and foreignness for the Man of the Enlightenment. Accounts of voyages were mostly written by Jesuit missionaries and flooded in during the first half of the century. One of the *Lettres édifiantes* written by Frère Attiret from Peking in 1743 describes the 'Garden of Gardens' at the Imperial Palace, saying 'one wants a beautiful disorder and asymmetry to reign over everything'. The author marvels at the miniature landscape, the sinuous lines of the footpaths adorned with pavilions and little grottoes and an artificial stream spanned by arched bridges, making way for little boats. These gardens also included menageries and fishponds. The 'Chinese', or 'Anglo-Chinese', element in the English garden also represented the grotesque side of an unsettling world, steeped with vertiginous cliffs, dreadful chasms, raging torrents and mountains with summits lost among the clouds, whose peaks back-lit the deformed silhouettes of trees tortured by storms, or strange monuments with horned roofs, decorated with bells and grimacing monsters. The garden conveyed an image of this strange country, thousands of leagues from the west, populated by people with morals and costumes as barbaric as they were refined. So far away and so idealized, it made it appear to be a nation which, through its wisdom, could reconcile the purity of the natural state with the benefits of one of the most highly complex civilizations. For Europe the Chinese empire was the embodiment of surprise and discovery, fear and admiration, agitation and excitement. From a design point of view it was also an inexhaustible mine of decorative motifs which European artists exploited to the full. The architect William Chambers, for example, published a collection of drawings of Chinese buildings in 1757. The book was mainly preoccupied with small garden buildings, bridges, pavilions and pagodas and drew to a close with the following words: 'The art of laying out gardens in the Chinese style is susceptible to as many variations as there are different arrangements in the work of Creation'. The problem is clear, the atheistic reference patently obvious: the work of Man, once more elevated to the status of demi-god, must equal the work of the Creator.

The second influence on the English style was Antiquity, which had always been a recurring theme in the history of Northern European and Italian architecture, by virtue of its historical importance and its availability, but the new garden style followed a very specific path, the pictorial vision of landscape painting. This was admired by the French, but generally considered to be secondary in importance to great allegorical or historical pictures. Collectors on the other side of the Channel, however, had developed a particular fondness for this genre through the work of a handful of seventeenth-century painters who were highly influenced by Italy and most of whom were trained in Rome. Among them were the Flemish artist Paul Brill, the Neapolitan Salvator Rosa, and the Frenchmen Gaspard Dughet, Claude Lorrain, master of luminous and limpid horizons, and Nicolas Poussin, whose arcadian landscapes were populated with shepherds in repose beside tombs concealed by greenery. These paintings supplied garden designers with a repertoire of models and material: profiles of mountains, mutilated trees, rocky cataracts, undulating rivers, abandoned temples, ruins, fountains and pyramids, as well as the shepherds and livestock which inhabited the foregrounds. The landscape designer borrowed the painter's techniques, from the initial framing of the image, the angles of the views, the depth of field, the layering of the planes, the view of the distance or the line of the horizon, to the distribution of masses and colours.

Successive waves of young French artists enriched this Italian vision of the garden during the middle years of the eighteenth century. Joseph Vernet's approach was precise and sensitive, Fragonard's fantastic and occasionally dishevelled, Valenciennes by contrast was theoretical and cool. The most influential of them all was Hubert Robert, a warm and extraordinarily prolific man, whose vivacious and brilliantly inventive efforts amount almost to 'a machine for producing landscape'. But the major themes created by Robert's cursive and vibrant hand were far from mere exercises in aesthetics, as abundant as they were superficial. Inspired by images of the Roman campagna reworked from sketches executed on site in incisive strokes of red chalk he churned out the same, never-changing vision in dozens of pictures. Much more powerful, much more influential than Poussin's ethereal paradise, Robert's vision was not of a glorious and triumphant born-again Rome, but quite the opposite, an Antique world only beautified through decay. It was a vision of a ruined imperial city strewn with abandoned temples and deserted altars, fallen statues of deities and shattered obelisks. The symbols of power and religion are deposed and re-used by rustics. Ignorant of the glories of the past, they see the ruins only as a setting for their daily lives and do not hesitate to reclaim the remains by training vines up them, by boarding up arcades and by building hovels of mud walls and thatched roofs amongst them.

The trunks of great trees blend with decapitated columns. The wild acanthus twines its leaves around the carved acanthus leaves on the recumbent capitals. Cows graze among the marbles. Fires lit by woodcutters smoke the coffered vaults of emply basilicas, while laundresses hail each other at the foot of a ruined bridge, laying out their washing to dry across its gigantic arch. Children, in the innocence of youth, play on tombs and in the rubble of collapsing sanctuaries. Here ivy and vines creep along cornices and architraves until eventually they find and wrap the effigies of long-forgotten divinities.

The image of these ruins reclaimed by modern life was neither sad nor nostalgic. On the contrary, it breathed peaceful well-being, wisdom and serenity. It invited the viewer to reflect on the passage of time, the vulnerability of empires, the vanity of passion and of human endeavour. It made a plea for the simpler merits of pastoral and rustic life, for taking each day as it came, forsaking ambition, and opting for a life whose sole enrichments were the lavish benefits provided, without cost, by Nature, and the emotions which it could excite in the human heart. The symbolism is obvious, the message direct. Where Poussin and Claude's Roman campagna was poetic, Robert's is philosophical, if not political. Power and religion are ephemeral; happiness lies elsewhere. Was the artist aware of the philosophy which runs through his work? In any case, at some point, it became a catalyst in the ferment of ideas which agitated the whole of society.

Jean-Jacques Rousseau contributed a determining moral dimension to this thinking by laying the foundations of a new ideal which reconciled sentiment and reason, as well as a new social order which advocated an enduring faith, optimistic or melancholic, but always unwavering, in the merits of Nature. The almost intuitive approach which the poet/philosopher brought to gardening corresponded perfectly to his ideology. The latter was disseminated over several years by a series of technical and doctrinal treaties, published in rapid succession in order to set out and spread the rules of this transfigured vision of landscape. The telling epigraph at the beginning of one of these works, edited by the Duc d'Harcourt who himself was a precurser of the new 'sensibility', sums up the theory of landscape with the words '*Ars est celare artem*' or 'Art lies in concealing art'. The garden is above all an artificial creation, a work of illusion; the more cunning the former, the more perfect the latter.

In 1774 the painter Claude-Henri Watelet published his own essay on gardens in which he developed ideas about separating out the various different 'sentiments': the poetic, picturesque or Romanesque genres, the noble, rustic, frivolous, sober or sad 'types', and started up a debate between painting and geometry, art and engineering, garden design and architecture. If the new movement proved itself to be particularly persuasive during these years, it was still far from unanimous in its views. On the contrary, it was the battleground for disagreement as well as debate.

Although the new garden theory at the time was based on a number of uniformly-held beliefs such as the rejection of the old dictates of symmetry and of coppicing and the imitation of nature, we can see with hindsight that there were two main lines of debate. The first divided into the extremists, partisans of the school of 'total irregularity', and the moderates, who, without actually defending the old style, still believed the immediate surroundings of the house must retain a certain symmetry. The second witnessed the often much more virulent confrontation between those who were unconditionally loyal to the entirely man-made 'theatrical' garden, a masterpiece of sham, often overloaded with machinery and effects such as mechanized cascades, chasms exhaling vapours, extravagant workmanship and exotic trees, and those who believed in leaving nature to be as natural as possible and parks as countrified.

This was achieved by minimal upkeep, undertaken discreetly and by enriching the existing landscape. The latter strand also opposed, in simplified terms, the 'Chinese' to the English style, the decorators to the landscapists, engineers to poets. Furthermore, town gardens were condemned on the basis that they were constrained by the meagreness and banality of their sites, but so were gardens in fields where nature had already dictated the lines of the composition.

Aged fourteen and a half, the young princess of Austria, torn from the bosom of her family and equipped with little more than a provincial education, arrived in France to be married, on 16 May 1770. Four years later, in 1774, she was crowned queen and immediately plunged into the heart of the debate which raged around her, and which seemed as though it was being fought by the most brilliant minds among Europe's scientific, artistic and aristocratic élite. A coterie of fantastically wealthy amateurs were locked in ruthless combat, arguing first about garden theory and then as they built on individual sites, such as the Parc Monceau, Ermenonville, Méréville and Maupertuis. They battled with each other with terraces, artificial grottoes and ruined pyramids, at great speed and at great expense.

It was inevitable that the queen's nearest and dearest, the royal family itself, would eventually become embroiled in this society phenomenon. People were giving in all around them, had given in, or were on the verge of giving in to this all-consuming Anglomania. The queen could not help but be a pioneer. At first timid and reserved, on her accession to the throne she enthusiastically followed suit with the means the affectionate king had put at her disposal. There could hardly have been a more appropriate place for her to pursue her ideas than the little estate at Trianon, of which she took possession on 6 June 1774. Louis XV's botanical garden with its thousands of incomprehensible Latin labels lined up in rows, lovingly expanded upon by Antoine Richard and his son, seemed very dull to her, crying out for something more up to date. So quite sensibly and still respectful of the rules currently in force, she turned to Richard, the incumbent gardener at Trianon, with her proposal for a new garden.

Antoine Richard was mortified by the iconoclasm which called into question his life's work, but ever the devoted servant, ready to satisfy his new mistress's slightest whim, he nevertheless endeavoured to come up with a design in the 'Anglo-Chinese' style, details of which he had studied on trips to Stowe and

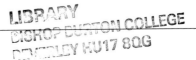

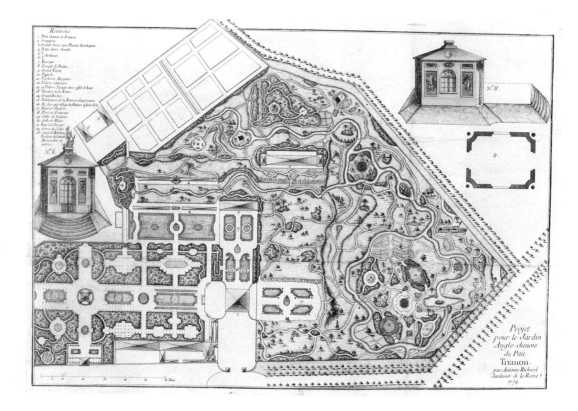

Kew. However, the queen's disappointed expression when she saw his impoverished design, with its overcomplicated and awkwardly zigzagging paths, decided the fate of the project at a stroke.

The Princesse de Beauvau, who sang the praises of an amateur called the Comte de Caraman, recommended him instead. Caraman's gardens for his *hôtel particulier* in the rue Saint-Dominique and his house at Roissy were prompting admiring responses from experts in the field. Engaged to this end by the queen, the count applied himself assiduously to the task and presented a much simpler, looser design on 10 July with long vistas and wide open spaces punctuated by little groups of trees unfolding beneath the windows of the palace, arranged around the graceful meandering line of an artificial river which undulated through grassy, flower-filled meadows. The queen instantly gave it her seal of approval and a contract with the count was signed on the 15 July. Caraman also had the honour to receive the queen in his garden in Paris, in order to give her a demonstration of his art. He received, in thanks, the title of Directeur des Jardins de la Reine and turned up at Trianon the following morning to launch the project.

Antoine Richard, Richard Mique and quite understandably, Hubert Robert, who was given the parallel title of Dessinateur des Jardins du Roi, competed

*Design for the 'Anglo-Chinese' garden at the Petit Trianon*

Antoine Richard, 1774

Although Antoine Richard may have resigned himself to the destruction of Louis XV's botanical garden, this unfulfilled design shows how he nevertheless cunningly attempted to spare the large greenhouses (see the plan for the original greenhouses on page 125).

*Plan of the queen's palace and garden at Trianon*

Richard Mique, 1779

The first Jardin anglais, laid out in accordance with Caraman's design between 1774 and 1782, unfolded to the east. Its spaciousness and curved outlines were diametrically opposed to the symmetrical framework and orthogonal lines of the Jardin français.

*Marie-Antoinette (1755-1793) and her children*

Adolphe-Ulric Wertmüller, 1785

The queen is portrayed in her Jardin anglais, accompanied by her daughter Marie-Thérèse-Charlotte, Madame Royale (1778-1851) and the Dauphin, Louis, who was born in 1781 and died in 1789.

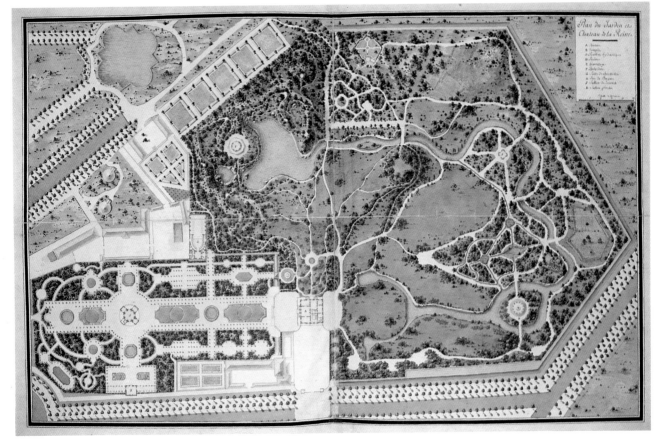

with each other to make their contribution to a task which they could see would be exceptional in every way. Richard selected the trees and rare plants, no longer chosen for their scientific interest but for their intrinsic beauty, while the others designed and finalized buildings and general composition.

By 1776 they had even succeeded in taking over the project, pushing Caraman, the amateur, to one side and placing Mique, the professional, in charge. The botanical collections were carefully transferred to the Jardin des Plantes in Paris.

The large greenhouse on the other hand was knocked down without any qualms to allow for the hollowing out of the sandy and porous soil to make the little upper lake and the river, and rubble from the excavation was used for banking up the artificial mountains. The river was lined with loam to make it watertight, giving rise to confusion over its name, the Rivière Anglaise, which also meant *en glaise* (loam). The mountains became the support and the setting for the series of 'barbaric' features: the Rocher, begun in 1779, the Grotte, the Ponts de Roches and the Montagne de l'Escargot, a steep, spiralling maze of paths, overshadowed by scientifically-ordered terraces of young pines, larches, firs and junipers, brought back by Richard from his alpine expeditions.

The Antique was also a source of inspiration. Initially there was going to be a ruin with four columns surrounded by the debris of what was assumed to have been the pediment but this image of destruction was considered too sad and was soon replaced by two much more seductive buildings. The first, opened on 3 September 1778, was an elegant rotunda, the Temple de l'Amour, which sat in the middle of a large island linked to the surrounding lawns by two bridges. This was followed by the Belvédère begun in the same year. It was an exquisite octagonal pavilion, a masterpiece of neo-classical perfection, guarded by eight carved sphinxes and, to contrast with the temple, was set elegantly on a rocky outcrop overlooking the upper lake.

The 'Chinese' element was not forgotten. However, instead of the pagoda, kiosks and aviary proposed by Richard at the outset, there was a 'Chinese' version of the ring game on a merry-go-round, *jeu de bagues*, to amuse the queen and her friends, inserted between the old Jardin français and the new Jardin anglais in 1776.

But one hue was still missing from the palette of different English genres, mountain, classical and 'Chinese'. It was the rustic. Fortunately a role model for this had been available at Chantilly since 1775, when the Prince de Condé

*Interior of the Trianon Grotto*

Claude-Louis Châtelet, 1786

The tiny grotto with the discreet staircase encouraged speculation and malicious gossip about the nature of the queen's distractions and pleasures at Trianon.

*The illumination
of the Rock and the Belvédère*

Claude-Louis Châtelet, 1781

'I thought I must be mad or dreaming' wrote the Duc de Cröy in 1780, when he saw large mountains, a huge rock and a river in place of the famous hot-houses that had been renowned throughout Europe. Never had two acres of ground been so altered, and at such a cost.

Fête de nuit *held by the queen*
*for the Comte du Nord,*
*at Trianon on 6 June 1782*

Hubert Robert, circa 1782

The queen received the crowned
heads of Europe at Trianon,
each under a different
pseudonym. Joseph II, Emperor
of Austria went in 1777 and
1780, Grand-Duke Paul of
Russia, the 'Comte du Nord',

went in 1782, King Gustav III
of Sweden in 1784 and the
Archduke Ferdinand of Austria
in 1786. On these occasions
the various attractions and views
in the Jardin anglais were
lit up for the evening, with
flaming torches stuck into
the ditches and Chinese lanterns
suspended from the branches
of the trees or hidden
among the clumps.

*View of the Petit Trianon
and the Temple de l'Amour*

Louis-Nicolas de Lespinasse,
circa 1780

Beneath the dome of the temple
stands a statue by Bouchardon,
'Cupid carving a bow from the
club of Hercules'. Further on,
just visible through the foliage,
is the exotic, pointed outline
of the central parasol of
the first 'Chinese'
*jeu de bagues.*

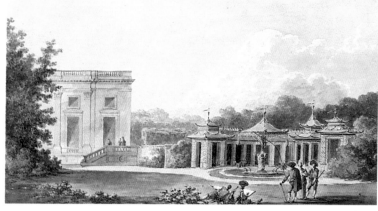

*Sketch for a chinoiserie building
for the Petit Trianon*

Richard Mique, circa 1775

*'Chinese' jeu de bagues*

Claude-Louis Châtelet, 1786

The first merry-go-round, created
in 1776, had a revolving platform
and a parasol, and was turned
by two servants who stood
in an underground tunnel.
In 1782 a semi-circular spectator's
gallery was added and covered
with a 'horned' roof.

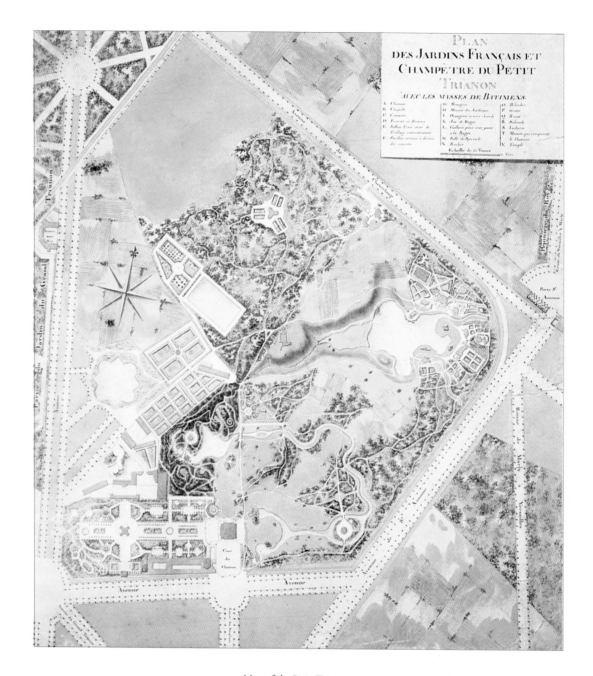

*Map of the Petit Trianon*

Richard Mique, 1786

The garden seen in this map has
attained its full size and links up
all the different types of garden:
Louis XV's Jardin français, the
Picturesque Jardin anglais with its
long vistas, the Queen's Hamlet
with its fan-like arrangement of
little fenced-in allotments, and the
Bois des Onze Arpents.

had built the Hameau, a kind of ornamental farm forming a tiny village or hamlet. Inspired by Condé's example, the queen annexed vacant land adjoining her own to the North, in the direction of the Bois des Onze Arpents. The tradition goes that it was Hubert Robert's idea, even though it was in fact Mique who drew up the plans in 1783.

The queen's Hamlet at Trianon was, it seems fair to say, entirely designed by Richard Mique. A pendant to the palace, a rustic village with eleven thatched cottages put to different uses (some were fake), a windmill, a dairy and a barn were interspersed with little vegetable patches and orchards fenced with stakes. The whole ensemble was displayed around a large lake which reflected the poplars and weeping willows planted along its banks.

The hamlet was built in a hybrid architectural style. The half-timbered façades of the buildings were clearly borrowed from Normandy, while the reed coverings, although also Norman, were common to most rustic dwellings in Northern Europe during the period, but the roofs which were covered with small tiles inset with dormer windows, and the plaster-covered rubble façades, were features of the Île-de-France. Finally, it was impossible to ignore the Flemish influence which showed through in the generous use of brick, 'sparrow-stepped' gables and the shutters with stained-glass window-panes, which conjured up the settings of the peasant *fêtes* and village feasts painted by Breughel and Teniers.

Thus the hamlet, like all the other attractions in the gardens, was an interpretive synthesis, a combination of styles which recaptured in real space the cutouts and the outlines of the hastily-painted canvas settings for the rustic operettas which the queen so enjoyed acting in at her little theatre. Its façades were packed with a profusion of galleries, balconies and rickety staircases, decorated with strings of blue-and-white faience pots, floating flowerbeds of wallflowers and geraniums which seemed made to complement romantic duos from comic opera.

The dilapidated-looking little cottages with their moss-covered roofs, their cracked façades and their frameworks painted to look like 'rotten wood', treated the privileged visitors who stepped over their thresholds to the startling 'cottage surprise'. On entering the little hovels they gasped in disbelief at the contrast between the 'decayed' look of the exteriors and the sumptuous interiors reserved for the queen's use, which shone with gold, silks and marbles, more suitable for the guests who came here to indulge in conversation, play cards or take supper.

### Earthenware flowerpot

Saint-Clément Potteries, 1785

Mique commissioned 1,232 blue-and-white flowerpots decorated with the queen's monogram, from the Saint-Clément Potteries in Lorraine (of which he was, incidentally, the majority shareholder). They were distributed around the houses and gardens of the Queen's Hamlet.

### The Queen's Hamlet

Claude-Louis Châtelet, 1786

Various buildings are arranged around the lake (from left to right): the preparation Dairy, the display Dairy, the Barn, the Fishing Tower and the Dovecote. On the other side of the river is the Billiard House, connected to the queen's house by a pergola, and finally, the Windmill.

### The Boudoir and the Windmill

Van Blarenberghe, 1786

Certain houses were reserved exclusively for the use of the queen and her guests. Others served as a backdrop against which farmers and servants worked, acting out the roles of the characters in a kind of animated rustic 'tableau vivant'.

The landscape which provided the idyllic setting was an extension of the original Jardin anglais. It cleverly blended its deep woods, its gushing streams, its fields of rye and wheat, rigorously striped by the furrowing of ploughs, and its undulating meadows dotted with blossoming groves and rare trees to create a new countryside. The walker's itinerary revealed views of the various attractions in this little enchanted paradise in unfolding succession, by cleverly alternating great swathes of thick shrubbery which masked the views with clusters of tall species through which they were glimpsed.

A ha-ha, the ditch invented by the English and known in French as *the saut-de-loup*, went round the entire garden, making it possible to prevent access without obscuring the view with a wall. It made it possible to see fragments of the 'real' countryside in the far distance through the rows of trees in the park. It annexed, visually, the fields of Chèvreloup, the meadows of the Ermitage and a few cottages huddled beneath the charming silhouette of the little chapel of Saint-Antoine-du-Buisson. Its belltower, seen in the distance from the side of the lake, was thus fitted into the composition of the theatrical village, giving Mique a rare chance to economize on a fake church whilst adding a convincing touch of truth to his fantasy landscape. But this last anchor in the real world soon became an embarrassment, a disagreeable reminder perhaps of the appalling misery inflicted on the French countryside by the cruel winters of the 1780s. A nobler feature, this time of Roman inspiration, was created on its doorstep in 1787 when the old gateway to Marly was transformed into a monumental triumphal arch.

There was only one thing which prevented this landscape of illusion being credible: the lack of people to give it scale, to give foreground interest and transform it into a real *tableau vivant*. To rectify this a little farm of about eleven acres was built near Blois and put into use in July 1785. It was stocked with cows imported from Switzerland, pigs and a herd of nanny-goats, sheep and goats, over whom reigned a white billy goat. It was also supplied with a herdsman, Valy Bussard, who arrived from the Touraine several days later, soon to be joined by his wife and two children, a manservant, a cowherd and a maid whose job was to bring the milk to the palace every morning. The farm also housed a Swiss Guard, Jean Bersy, and a garden boy. And so the farm was brought to life by the gossip of laundrymaids at the mill, the shouts of reapers in the hay, the sound of doves taking flight, the spectacle of ploughing or of livestock grazing on the lawns, in an animated *tableau champêtre*, an eternal pastorale.

The queen, dressed in modest country garb, was fond of walking here with her children. Like a châtelaine inspecting her land, she would visit and explore the households of humble families with their smoky interiors and their patriarchal ways which contrasted so starkly with the taffetas and frivolities which were the stuff of her own daily life. To her these people looked as though they had stepped straight out of a painting by Le Nain or Greuze and thus appeared even closer to an idealized state of Nature.

But the unnaturally natural garden and the theatrical hamlet must not be dismissed as a marginal or subsidiary episode, a futile waste of money, in the history of art and of France itself. It is true that Trianon was less romantic than Bagatelle, less 'Chinese' than Cassan, less literary and less English than Ermenonville, less antique even than Maupertuis, less esoteric than the Désert de Retz, less extensive finally, and a lot less costly, than Méréville, but it was undoubtedly the most complete, the most elegant, the most perfect French example of the gardens set out in the English style in the dying years of the Ancien Régime. The best preserved, it has become an extraordinarily moving reminder of an era which we cannot grasp, and does the most to conjure up before our eyes the various parts of this multifaceted art which enjoyed such a brief, but full, apotheosis.

Some are inclined to see the Jardin anglais as little more than the perfect product of the encyclopedist movement. It certainly was an eclectic survey of arts, styles, plants and techniques. It did conduct scientific experiments with new agricultural and cultivation processes (the Queen's Hamlet at Trianon, which was a kind of experimental farm, undoubtedly played a role in this). Its development of engineering seemed to rival the Creator's. Mechanics vied over the building of waterfalls, rivers and mountains which were truly 'larger than life'. The Voltairian, atheistic idea was pursued to its logical conclusion by diluting and diffracting the divine image through a multitude of temples to the god Pan, to Love, Peace and Filial Piety, and by only ever portraying churches in ruins. Thus the Jardin anglais placed Man firmly at the centre of the universe.

Others take the opposite view. They interpret the naive pursuit of regeneration through rural life, the sentimental idealization of Nature's bounties and the power of Jean-Jacques Rousseau's new deity, the Supreme Being, as a preromantic literary reflection on the hopelessness of human endeavour and the vanity of ephemeral power, an escape into the imagination, a sliding towards a dream state by means of a deliberate confusion of reality and all its modes of its representation.

But this queen, soon to be accused of having scandalously played at being a shepherdess while her subjects were dying of hunger in the countryside less than a league from Trianon, did she have a sense of foreboding? Did the élite, either ignorant or indifferent to the point of provocation to the sufferings of the people, mindful only of their own privileges and who surrounded the queen, only to distract her, sense the inexorable evolution of the drama which was coming? Did they really believe that the last happy days of the reign of Louis XVI could last for ever when a worrying feeling of injustice and revolt was growling all around them? Did they see the abyss opening up in front of them or did they pretend to ignore it in order to make the most of a month, a day, an hour, the last flickering embers of a happiness which was slipping through their fingers? The last moments were the most pleasurable, the most precious also, because they were the most fragile. Once the spell was broken they were thrown brutally towards the torments of exile, the scaffold and dreadful betrayal.

Did it not occur to this tiny aristocracy that its ruinous mania for gardening, the ultimate dance on top of the smouldering volcano, the last fleeting pleasure before the fall, was like the most painful form of unbearable inner conflict? They were the possessors of power which could no longer be guaranteed, summoned by an ethereal longing for progress, but manifestly incapable of renouncing the slightest privilege or pleasure. Did they realize that it was a kind of suicidal schizophrenia driven either by fecklessness, lassitude or premonition?

The hunt, which had presided over the birth of Versailles all those years ago, was in progress on the day of its demise, 5 October 1789. Louis XVI was shooting at Meudon when he was informed, in haste, of the deputation of rabble en route to Versailles from Paris to seize the king. The queen, only recently so popular, was out walking alone, a solitary figure strolling up and down the paths of her enchanted garden; she enjoyed the apparent calm of the autumn afternoon, even though the weather was overcast and brought rain that evening. No doubt she was unable to chase the sad memories of the summer from her mind, when the Dauphin had died and her closest friends had begun to keep their distance and then to escape, signalling the emigration which left her alone to face the storm which was shortly to crush her. A female

*The entrance to
the Trianon Grotto*

Claude-Louis Châtelet, 1786

servant, sent from the palace to warn her of the riot and to persuade her to return to Versailles now that the mob was already at the gates, found her 'sitting in her grotto, sunk in melancholy reflection'.

The quarry in the hunt at Versailles had changed. Today it was the monarchy which found itself ensnared in the trap, the sovereigns who had become the prey and the queen, who departed in haste with a rustle of silk across the rocks, wrenched from her cool little grotto, like an animal from its lair. Thus this grotto became the dynasty's very last retreat at the end of a succession of lines of retrenchment — Versailles, Marly, Trianon, the Queen's Hamlet — inserted between themselves and their subjects by the monarchs. It seems with hindsight that, little by little, they had begun to seek nothing more in their gardens than a place of escape, where they could flee from the obligations and responsibilities of power, a kind of gradual abdication in the face of the heavy weight of their lot. But while her lively step followed the paths which wound around the edges of the lake on the eve of her downfall, one wonders whether Marie-Antoinette had a final thought for her unfinished garden, for this last piece of workmanship which her days, now remorselessly numbered, did not leave her time to see completed. Still further from prying eyes, even further withdrawn from a world where time was relentlessly catching up with her, did she ultimately find solitude in the last refuge, hidden behind the Queen's Hamlet, in the depths of the elegiac and Virgilian Bois des Onze Arpents, designed by Mique to her own specification?

With the interruption of building work at the Trianon in 1789, tradesmen's bills amounting to nearly half a million *livres* were left unpaid. The inefficiency of the Bâtiments du Roi, which was often slow to honour the accounts which it was presented with, does not explain everything. That suppliers deliberately delayed submitting invoices seems to have been a roundabout way, by advancing credit to the crown, of luring future commissions as compensation, at prices which they all hoped to cash in on in the end. However, when events began to speed up and the risk that they might never get paid began for the first time to look very real, these obsequious tradesmen promptly started brandishing their unpaid bills, like certificates of republicanism, and claiming to be the 'victims' of the 'Austrian's' profligacy. Instruments of propaganda themselves, public opinion credited them with the thesis that it was the gardens, the rocks, the river, the hamlet and the little grotto that had frittered away scandalous amounts of money, ruining the kingdom and bringing it to its present state of misery. This little estate was the real cause of all the grievances.

History will probably never be able to determine whether it was just, or unjust, to blame the delights of the Trianon for the shortsightedness of an entire dynasty and the accumulation of so many years of suffering and injustice towards the people. In focusing all its attacks on the queen's property, undoubtedly falsifying the truth, by creating a formidable ideological tool which benefited a genuine political manifesto, the revolutionary tribunal played a final role in the garden, something which had certainly never been envisaged by its creators. In forging the lever which allowed the new age to reverse the crumbling old order, the unpaid bills of the Trianon were a way of paying for two centuries of absolutism.

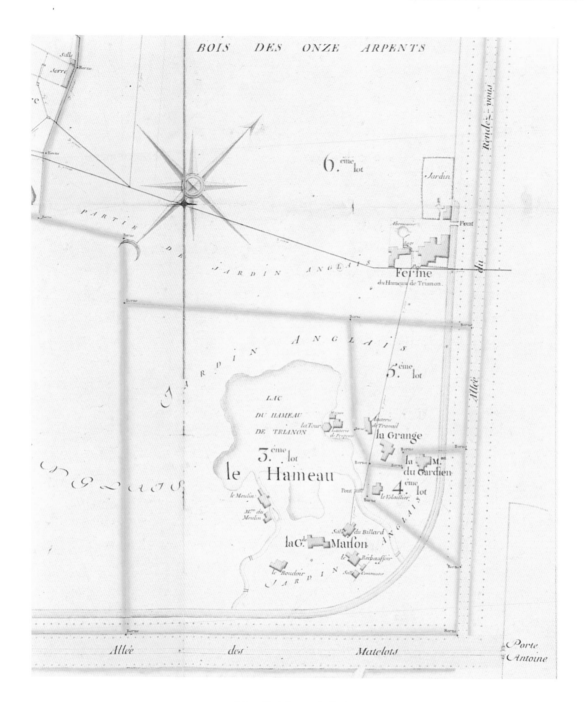

*Map of sale lots at the Petit Trianon,* detail

Delacroix,
Germinal, Year III, 1795

In 1795 the gardens of the Petit
Trianon and the Queen's Hamlet
were divided into ten lots. Their
sale was, however, postponed
by Antoine Richard, former
gardener to Marie-Antoinette.

# The Tree of Liberty

It is easy to imagine that Versailles, deserted by the king, was immediately abandoned and vandalized, but this was not the case. The rupture was not brutal. For months between 1789 and 1792, a cohort of civil servants and palace officials tacitly awaited an imaginary return of the court, as though the events taking place in Paris were no more than a passing phase and the royal family's stay at the Tuileries a straightforward, recurring part of the royal itinerary. In a town where the palace was the main source of employment, the best means of safeguarding jobs was to continue to run the palace, thus minimizing the shock caused by the transition.

But the king's execution, on 21 January 1793, put an end to these last hopes. There was talk of ploughing up the garden, of giving it over to agriculture, a just repayment to the peasants of Galie, who had been dispossessed of their land for more than two centuries, as though the whole thing had been no more than a parenthesis in the history of a peaceful country area in the Île-de-France.

The vision of labourers working at the foot of the ruined palace was in the spirit of an era whose dreams Hubert Robert had so convincingly illustrated. The fantasy, heavy with moral overtones, was apt and bound to arouse emotions.

In the end a more prosaic solution was found. The Convention and the minister Roland decided to make commercial use of crown property and sold the furniture at auction. This lasted from August 1793 to August 1794. In the same year the collections of paintings were dispersed, metals requisitioned for the arsenal and the mint, trees in the woods felled and land in the Grand Parc distributed.

The Petit Trianon, imbued with such potent symbolism, was sacked and at first even put up for sale. Antoine Richard, the queen's old gardener and a wily tactician, had recently converted to Republicanism and managed to obtain new powers under the title of Directeur des Jardins Botaniques de Trianon. He persuaded the Convention to issue a decree declaring the need to preserve the houses and gardens, at the expense of the Republic, 'for the delight of the people and to create institutions of use to agriculture and the arts'. These noble objectives were met by granting a lemonade-seller called Langlois the right to transform the Petit Trianon into an hotel, the Pavillon français into a café and Gabriel's lovely French garden into an open air ballroom.

Richard's proposal to make Versailles yield revenue by converting the parterres into vegetable gardens and planting the borders of the pools and the Grand Canal with orchards gave concrete expression to the second objective. By the end of 1783, fruit trees could be seen growing at the foot of the château, on the quincunxes and the esplanade of the Bassin d'Apollon. The banks of the Canal were partly demolished in 1795 to allow for drainage, divided into three lots and converted into pasture. The trees in the copses and the avenues were also felled for the use of the army and the navy. Richard, who had devoted himself lovingly to the preservation and upkeep of the hothouses at Trianon and to their precious botanical collections, was responsible for postponing their sale. Indeed they were not safe until a central school was founded at Versailles (whose experimental garden was in Richard's care) precipitating their removal to the kitchen garden, for students to study.

The gardens were more or less officially open to the public. Thirteen citizens and eight guards were allowed to show people round the bosquets, which were normally under lock and key. The uses to which the gardens were put nevertheless became increasingly debased, typified by the presence of soldiers' wives, in the month of Ventose in Year IV of the Republic, 'washing their linen in the *buffet d'eau*, on either side of the terrace, beating it on the marble tablets and hanging it out to dry on the branches of the hornbeam along the walks'.

The next episode in the dreamt-of return to agriculture, an invasion of the garden into the town, was fuelled in 1794 when most of the paving stones of

*The warden's house
at the Queen's Hamlet*

John-Claude Nattes, circa 1802

The cottages at the Queen's Hamlet were flimsily built out of light-weight materials, hence they suffered a good deal when they were abandoned during the revolutionary period. The little gardens, also abandoned, were choked with weeds.

*The Queen's Hamlet
at the Petit Trianon*

Pierre-Joseph Wallaert, 1803

The Queen's Hamlet was now partly ruined and overgrown with vegetation. Its pastures had been rented to a farmer. Foreigners and the inquisitive sometimes ventured along its paths to visit the Tower, the Billiard House, the Queen's House and the Boudoir, the fragile remains of the late queen's secret domain.

the Cour d'Honneur in front of the palace were dug up and the area wash sown with four squares of grass. In Year V a certain Machaux even went so far as to ask for permission to graze his flocks here but the ultimate act of iconoclasm was committed on 21 January 1798. A tree of liberty was planted at the centre of the courtyard under the very windows of the Chambre du Roi, in celebration of the fifth anniversary of the execution of Louis XVI.

However, neither Liberty nor its tree was to survive for long. The visits made by Napoleon I and the Empress Josephine on 13 and 22 March 1805 put an end to these Rousseauesque ravings, by compensating or evicting all unofficial lodgers and occupants. The emperor had been considering the idea of a return of power to Versailles for some time and doubtless continued to play with the idea. In the end he settled on the use of Trianon as a private residence for himself and his family but the art of gardening was not one of

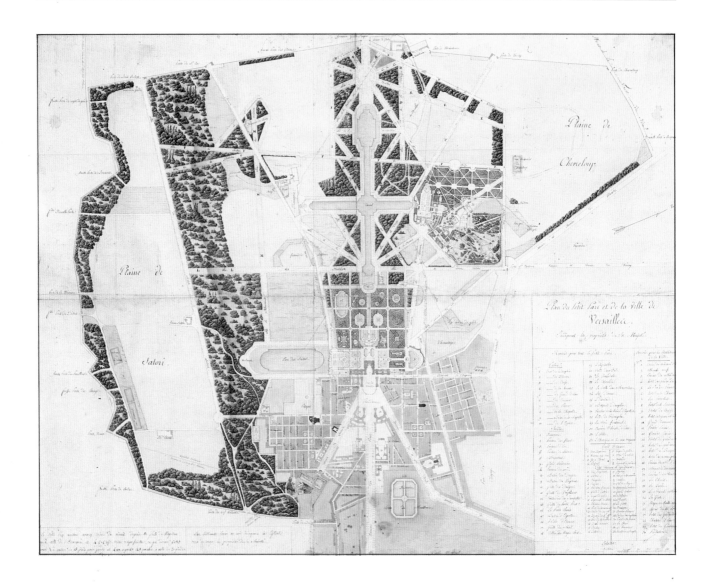

Napoleon's higher priorities. His alterations, which were spartan and uncom-
promisingly military in character, were motivated by only two main criteria.
The first was economy. The emperor set aside a mere 120,000 francs for the
restoration of the gardens at Trianon and 80,000 francs for the gardens at Versailles, while he did not hesitate to provide a budget of 300,000 francs alone
for the refurnishing of the two Trianon palaces.

Contemporary plans show that Louis XVI's simplification of the original outlines completed 30 years earlier had already been eroded by ten years of
neglect. The large compartmentalized parterres, the Parterre de l'Orangerie,
the Parterre de Latone and the Parterres du Grand Trianon, had been simplified, reduced to their main orthogonals, only enriched by huge circular
flowerbeds. The vestiges of the bosquets at the Arc de Triomphe and the

*Map of the Petit Parc and the town of Versailles, indicating His Majesty's property*

1807-10

Napoleon I pursued a policy of non-compulsory recovery of the core of the former royal domains, which had been partly broken up by the sales of the Revolutionary period. The Petit Parc is here seen surrounded by farm holdings and the dependencies of Satory, Gally and Chèvreloup.

*The clearing in front of the Grand Trianon*

Jean-Joseph Bidauld and Carle Vernet, 1810

Napoleon appropriated Trianon and often went to stay there. Easily identified by his white horse and his colonel's uniform, he rides towards the Allée de Bailly, followed by three chamberlains and an Egyptian, Roustan.

Trois Fontaines were cut down, the Pavillon frais in the Jardin français at Trianon had been demolished along with its charming trelliswork gallery, its pools and parterres destroyed. The fragile remaining features were subjected to the most drastic simplifications.

Napoleon's second concern was for security. The assassination attempt in the rue Saint-Nicaise in Paris on 24 December, or 3 Nivose in the Year IX, when the First Consul only narrowly escaped an explosion caused by a bomb which had been planted in a cart, showed the strength of opposition towards the new Establishment. To overcome such threats in the future, the emperor decided to unite the Grand Trianon and the Petit Trianon by building a wooden bridge across the Chemin Creux created to replace the old walk which had until then separated the two parks. He surrounded all this with a

*The Billiard House and the Queen's House at the Hamlet*

French School, circa 1811

While the Hamlet was being restored for the Empress Marie-Louise, the temporary stage scenery of the various houses was subject to specific alterations. The two exterior staircases at the Billiard House, for example, have been removed and a covered staircase inserted to the north. The thatched roofing of the pergola unites the two houses and the ruined fake tower to the south.

*The Fishery Tower and the display Dairy*

French School, circa 1811

The Tower's exterior staircase has been put back in its original position and the neighbouring Dairy, denuded of its marble decorations during the Revolution, has been redesigned.

continuous high fence punctuated with gates controlled by pavilions manned by porters and guards. He also extended this plan to the south-east by annexing part of the Grand Parc to create a forecourt to prevent vehicles from driving too close to the palaces.

To facilitate surveillance he cleared the views with a loose, picturesque network of wide curving avenues, for rides in barouches, which cut through huge carpets of meadow completely devoid of shrubbery but punctuated with clumps of ornamental beeches, pines and thujas. Napoleon had little personal taste in garden matters, little love for gardens and he was not prepared to invest much in the whole business. As far as he was concerned gardens were for women which explains why most of the work undertaken at the Grand Trianon in 1805 was done to receive Madame Mère; the gardens at the Petit Trianon were reserved for his sister, the Princesse Borghèse, and the restoration of the Queen's Hamlet was undertaken for his second wife, Empress Marie-Louise, Marie-Antoinette's niece.

The late queen's spruce little rustic village was in a pitiable state. After so many years of neglect, roofs had fallen in, exterior staircases had collapsed and

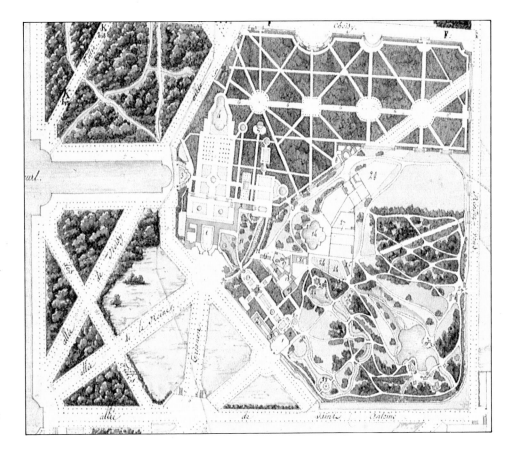

*Map of the Petit Parc and the town of Versailles, indicating His Majesty's property,* detail

1807-10

The park appears as it was under the Empire. We can see the road between the two Trianons, and the vast landscaped park stretching out in front of the palaces, to which Louis-Philippe later added a Hippodrome. The little gardens at the Queen's Hamlet have gone, along with the most dilapidated buildings.

the farm had been partly burnt down. Buildings deemed beyond repair were demolished without further ado. No attempt was made to recultivate the little gardens, vegetable patches and orchards which had long since lain fallow. They were replaced instead by a banal essay in the English style, which made the surviving thatched cottages look like knick-knacks laid out on the grass. The cottages were restored, redecorated and refurnished, and on 25 August 1811 the hamlet was reopened for the Empress's *fête.* Chinese lanterns were strung up and for a few hours village dramatists and choirs of children made a clumsy attempt at conjuring up the splendours, the extravagances and the magic of the final years of the Ancien Régime.

Louis XVIII, the former Comte de Provence and Louis XVI's younger brother, finally succeeded to the throne in 1815 and made his own attempt at reinstating Versailles as a seat of power but perhaps he knew too much about its traps and was too haunted by its ghosts to bring the necessary commitment to the task. The only legacy left to the gardens by his fleeting stay was the Jardin du Roi, designed by Dufour, the palace architect, in 1817. This was built over the old Île Royale ornamental lake, which had been partly filled in during the Empire.

Inscribed within a square frame defined by peripheral paths, this truly English 'square', oddly reminiscent of the king's emigration to London, surrounded the great oval of its concave lawn with a border of flowering shrubs shaded by rare trees. It also incorporated a number of borders where generations of gardeners have devoted themselves unrestrainedly to extremely detailed, multi-coloured planting patterns.

Louis-Philippe was the only one of the nineteenth-century heads of state to mastermind a real project. The Versailles of the new 'king of the French people' was no longer a private residence retained for the king's pleasure, neither was it the seat of power. It was no more than the symbol, the attestation of direct descent, the guarantor and the museumified expression of legitimacy. The minutes of onsite meetings held by the architect Nepveu record 398 visits made by the king in person to Versailles, in order to supervise the tiniest details of the enormous task of transforming the palace into an historical museum dedicated 'to the glory of France'. He seems to have made less than a dozen visits, on the other hand, to discuss the garden.

While the apartments in the wings were turned upside down and emptied from top to bottom without a second thought, and a vast programme of redecoration for the château was initiated, practically nothing was done to the park during his entire reign of eighteen years. The sole innovations were the Hippodrome at the Trianon, a timid attempt at replanting the Allée Saint-Antoine for which Nepveu was given a stiff reprimand by the king on the grounds that it was premature and over-ambitious, and the removal of the statues in the Bosquet des Dômes to Saint-Cloud. Louis-Philippe had little to show where the gardens were concerned.

His museum was above all a propaganda exercise, a rewriting of history with a bias towards the monarchy. It emphasized certain historic facts, certain flaws in the characters of one or other of his ancestors in order to redeem another.

*Panoramic view of the gardens at Versailles*

John Vanderlyn, 1818-19

Forty years on, the new trees in the bosquets have now reached maturity. Alterations carried out under the Empire, even though designed to preserve the scale and the views of Le Nôtre's garden, show how the line of the Parterre de Latone, the avenues of yew and the positioning of peripheral edges, have been markedly simplified and refined.

*The Parterre d'Eau*

Richard Parkes Bonington, circa 1826

The famous English landscape artist, best-known for his seascapes, created a novel view of the gardens of Versailles, most of which were now open to the public.

It is to Louis-Philippe in part that we owe the great legends of Versailles such as the undoubtedly exaggerated emphasis on the sacredness of Louis XIII's first château. The House of Orléans, to which Louis-Philippe belonged, was descended from Louis XIII's second son and was the traditional rival to the House of Bourbon. Louis-Philippe's father, Philippe Égalité, had conspired against Louis XVI and adopted republican ideas during the Revolution. Louis-Philippe therefore emphasized the legitimacy of his line on the one hand and undermined the authority of the Sun-King's successors on the other. Louis XV was caricatured as fickle and debauched; only capable of reigning from a corner of his bedroom, Louis XVI as a dimwitted locksmith, Marie-Antoinette as a frivolous shepherdess, more Austrian than French, and the last Bourbons gout-stricken incompetents, puppets reinstated and

controlled by foreign powers. Louis-Philippe rehabilitated the reputations of
the revolutionaries of 1789 and 1830, for having rid the world of this bloodless
line, and exalted the imperial armies which had conquered and civilized Europe,
thus securing the goodwill or neutrality of the republican and bonapartist
opposition.

The skilful reshaping and reinterpretation of history served, according to the
expression used by Guizot in 1830, 'to place the fleurs-de-lys of the Bouvines
on the flag of Austerlitz'. The king, product of an executed royal line, a former émigré and a hero of the barricades, manipulated the message with great
cunning.

The history of the gardens was subjected to an analagous, though far more
modest and less calculating, reinterpretation. This did not result, as we have

*A concert held in the Bosquet de la Colonnade*

Eugène Lami, 1861

Attempts to conjure up the splendours of the Grand Siècle in a resuscitated and museumified Versailles were a source of fascination to the artists of the second half of the nineteenth century, and gave this painter an opportunity to create a dazzling and idealized evocation of the spirit of the seventeenth century.

*The Fontaine de la Pyramide and the Allée d'Eau*

Mid-nineteenth century

The chestnut trees planted during the reign of Louis XVI are once again being pollarded in the old *marquise* style. Their heavy branches overhang the *palissades*. The parterres are once more embellished with alternating cone-shaped yews and flowering shrubs.

already seen, in great works, but in the daily business of maintaining, 'correcting' and embellishing the creations of former eras, in poor adjustments such as the replacement of the sandy paths with lawn, the introduction of flowers to compositions which formerly had none, and incongruous poplars, conifers and rare trees. All in all there was a bland balancing of French and English taste, and historical exactitude was almost completely sacrificed.

Nevertheless, Nature's cycle continued. Trees planted under Louis XVI achieved maturity under the Second Empire, were felled, and new ones planted in their place by the architect Questel. Planting began at the Bassin d'Apollon in 1860, with diagonal avenues of limes which descended to the Bassin des Saisons, and continued with the planting of plane trees along the cross paths in 1862-63. They were affected by a hurricane in 1870 which devastated the old avenues along the former Allée Royale, now known as the Allée du Tapis Vert. But this cruel incident was the harbinger of something worse, the Prussians at the gates of the capital, the withdrawal of the provisional government to Versailles, the Paris Commune; hundreds of 'federates' were incarcerated in the orangery, judged in the stables, and many of them shot on the wooded slopes of Satory. The Tapis Vert did not receive its new chestnut trees until 1876, when it was attended to during part of a general replantation programme completed in 1883.

Once firmly in place, the Third Republic affirmed the symbolism of Versailles by maintaining it as a place of assembly. The Bassin de Neptune — its lead decorations completely remade for the event — was the setting for a great public *fête* on 5 May 1889, held in honour of the centenary of the calling of the States General in 1789, in the presence of President Carnot.

What now remains of the different aspects given to the gardens by successive sovereigns, the slice of the natural world which Louis XIV imagined he had mastered, and towards which Louis XV was more of an observer and Louis XVI more ambivalent? What is the legacy of those hundred winters? What is left of their infinitely various additions and their different modes of formation? Finally, what remains of the Versailles whose essential qualities were altered progressively by the natural processes, fluctuations in taste, ideological discourse and economic constraints?

*View of the gardens, the château and the town of Versailles*

Deroy, Second Empire

The artist has depicted each bosquet and its fully-grown vegetation in exhaustive detail, in imitation of the great seventeenth-century perspectives by Israël Sylvestre.

*The Bust*

Henri Le Sidaner, autumn 1933

Many of the artists, poets and visitors who came to Versailles in the early years of the twentieth century proved themselves to be sensitive to the melancholy sight of the gardens, now deserted and abandoned, and exuding an incomparable atmosphere of nostalgia.

27. Parc de **VERSAILLES** — Rampe nord du parterre de Latone

*The north slope of the Parterre de Latone*

Postcard, circa 1900

The park at Versailles was now maintained as a public park. Its avenues of old yews were clipped in memory of the elaborate topiary created two centuries earlier by Le Nôtre and his gardeners.

# Regrowth and Renewal

Another century has passed in the history of the parterres, the bosquets and the woods at Versailles. The Republic did not have to take the Versailles of the kings by force, but first as a museum, where painstaking research was undertaken to restore a more faithful version of history, then as an historic monument classed as a former royal estate, even though it is the Bâtiments Civils and the Palais Nationaux, parallel organizations, which fund upkeep and repairs. We have witnessed a century of restoration projects, not all of which ended happily. One notable example was the replanting of the Petit Parc in 1924, abandoned in the face of public opposition, costing Chaussemiche, the Architect-in-chief, his job. Others such as his successor Patrice Bonnet's restoration of the houses, gardens and orchards at the Hamlet, carried out between 1930 and '34, were an unqualified success. With hindsight, some projects can be regarded as interpretations rather than restorations such as treatments of the parterres and their yew avenues by architects with an excessively 'modern' and pure vision but whose rigour is curiously tempered by a sometimes over-abundant profusion of flowers such as red salvia, calceolaria, maritime cineraria, geraniums and begonias.

The twentieth century has been the century of the visitor. Versailles has become a public garden. The first tourists were soldiers, off-duty for a few hours in what is after all a garrison town, nannies and children, and visitors happy to hire out deckchairs and enjoy the views of the garden. The gardens of Versailles belong primarily to the citizens of Versailles who have their own names for its different parts. The former Jardin has become the Petit Parc; what was the Petit Parc is now the Grand Parc. The Parterre du Nord is known as Petite Provence, the Rond Vert has been nicknamed the 'nannies' bosquet' and the sculptural group at the Bassin d'Apollon is often referred to as the 'mud-wagon'!

Also the gardens have seen another century of growth. The trees planted under the Third Republic are now a hundred years old and have passed the age of the hundred-year replanting cycle: 1675, 1775, 1875. The time is ripe for renewal but decisive action has been avoided year after year, partly because of the costs involved, but also because the park is now surrounded by an almost completely urban environment and the strength of public feeling about it runs very high. Perhaps most important of all is the fact that nostalgia, and appreciation of their symbolic value, prevented everyone from accepting that such huge and venerable trees must be felled even though they were obviously dilapidated. In the end the elements, the forces of Nature which Louis XIV once believed he could enslave, took their revenge. On 3 February 1990 a storm stuck, creating havoc. It took only several hours for high winds to fell more than 1,300 trees in the park and cause widespread damage to the garden. Countless trees were left seriously weakened and destabilized, or exposed by the disappearance of the trees which had screened them. The vegetation in

*The Bassin de Neptune and the north façades of the château*

Yves Breton, 1994

The felling of the trees in the two north bosquets, which took place in 1991, opened up a monumental view of the château from the Bassin de Neptune. A fourth generation of saplings, alternating with topiary and the Fontaines des Marmousets, frame the new Allée d'Eau, returned to its orginal state.

*Design for the restoration of the Bosquets du Nord: cross-section of the Bassin du Dragon and the Allée d'Eau*

Pierre-André Lablaude, 1991

The part of the gardens recently selected for replanting was favoured with a return to its state in the years 1700-15, girded by the architectural *palissades* of the bosquets planted with low woods, thus allowing distant views of the park from the terraces above.

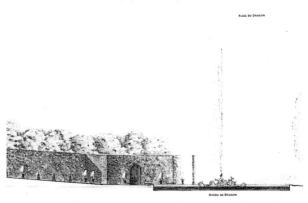

the bosquets, which had been slowly collapsing, besieged by the fatal diseases of old age for the past twenty years, was particularly vulnerable. The current generation was left with no option but to fell all the remaining trees in the Petit Parc and create new plantations over the course of the next twenty years. How then, after so many centuries of successive transformations, is it possible to experience the original gardens of Versailles? How can one comprehend, acknowledge a work of art as patrimonial as this, when it is composed of a material which must be replaced every century, which renews itself every spring, if not every day, which will mask the horizon, curtail the views and choke the main axes if it is not checked, to the point of self-obliteration?

How can one reconcile or validate the wholesale massacre of ephemeral architecture, the decorations in the bosquets of the Dômes, the Trois Fontaines and the Encelade, the porticoes of trelliswork in the Jardin français at Trianon, or the workmanship at the Queen's Hamlet, elements of which reveal themselves, nevertheless, every time excavation work is undertaken? How can we resign ourselves to seeing dried-up pools and fountains, or continue to make visitors believe that the parterres laid out last century, the Parterre de l'Orangerie, the Parterre de Latone or the Parterres at Trianon, were really created for Louis XIV?

But above all, how can we ignore hundreds of paintings, drawings and engravings, masterpieces by the great masters, or exhaustive renderings by uninspired artists, who nevertheless made up for their shortcomings with a scrupulous precision which is just as valuable to historians and scholars? Architectural projects, clumsy sketches by joint contractors jotted down in support of bills, surveyors' lists, designs or details of designs for fountains, hundreds of viewpoints provided by different professions and personalities throughout the ages — even though they often contradict each other over certain points, each one nevertheless sheds a certain light on the positioning of something or other, the outline of a bank or the shape of a piece of topiary, the lines of a design, a colour or a species. This body of material which has been amassed and deciphered has added immeasurably to the sum of knowledge which has gradually redefined and brought back to life with fantastic precision the outlines and details of work which was long ago destroyed or altered completely. Like the scores and crossed-out scores of rediscovered pieces of music, they beckon us to attempt a minute and faithful restoration. They demand to be respected, loved, and above all studied, not only the drawings and plans, archives and accounts, but also the garden, the seasons, the waters, the growth rate of the trees. The process of researching the history and meaning of all this work is never-ending. There are scientific, symbolic and imaginative dimensions to the gardens at Versailles which are still as yet largely unexplored, and still much is to be gained from studying the marble statuary. Oaks, chestnuts, ash and limes crash to the drone of the chain-saw. Hundreds of dead trees are being chopped down every winter, in successive screens, bosquet by bosquet, the tops of the trees exploding onto the ivy-covered carpet of the undergrowth. By contrast thousands of slender hornbeam, field maples and common linden grow higher with every passing spring; a profusion of young trees bursting out to take over where their elders left off.

*The Parterre du Nord and the North Wing*

Even though the shapes of the topiary and the techniques which created it have evolved considerably over the centuries, the Parterre du Nord still retains its original outlines, laid out between 1663 and 1666.

*The interior of the orangery*

Thousands of orange trees have succeeded each other under these vaults. The most venerable of them all was called Connétable. It was planted in 1421 at Pamplona, acquired by François I for Fontainebleau and transferred to Versailles by Louis XIV. It survived for two centuries, a venerable old man handled with great care by many generations of solicitous gardeners.

*The Parterre d'Eau*

This parterre reflects the sky and the façades of the château just as it did three centuries ago.

### The Parterre de l'Orangerie

The parterre appears to our eyes in its nineteenth-century garb, its squares framed by brightly-coloured flowerbeds. The two flights of steps known as the Cent Marches protect the plants in containers, brought out in spring, from cross-winds. They still tower over the orange trees as well the palm trees which also play an important role in the garden.

### The royal kitchen garden and the cathedral

The kitchen garden, at the heart of the old Saint-Louis quarter, still continues to produce exotic varieties of fruit and vegetables.

*The château, the orangery
and the Pièce d'eau des Suisses*

*View towards the west*

The overgrown bosquets planted
during the last century block the
background. The depth of the
gradations in the view which
Le Nôtre intended is no longer
visible except from the roof of the
château. However, the planes
do still align with the Parterre
d'Eau, the Parterre de Latone,
the Tapis Vert, the Grand Canal
and the foliage of the Grand Parc
on the horizon.

*Castor and Pollux*

Antoine Coysevox (1685-1712)

*The Bassin de Flore*

The avenues planted between 1986 and 1989 along the Allées des Saisons grow more like the green geometric *palissades* of the Grand Siècle with every passing year.

*The warden's house at the Queen's Hamlet*

*The Pavillon français and the Jardin français at the Petit Trianon*

Gabriel's composition was replanted in 1992, incorporating the final alterations to the parterres carried out prior to the Revolution.

*The Lake
and the Queen's Hamlet*

Scrupulously restored in the
1930s by the architect Patrice
Bonnet, according to the original
plans, the Queen's Hamlet is
indisputably the place which best
evokes the spirit of capriciousness
and insouciance which
characterized the last years
of the Ancien Régime.

*The meadows and walks
in the Grand Parc*

The depths of the Grand Parc to
the west of the Grand Canal still
retain miraculously preserved
fragments of the original,
untouched countryside out of
which Louis XIII created the first
garden, for his little hunting
lodge, more than 350 years ago.

The area surrounding the château is taking shape, restored to how it was at the end of Louis XIV's reign, complete with the striking walls of greenery so characteristic of the work of Le Nôtre. The work of the old gardener, dead for nearly three centuries, is the greatest asset with which we can equip the garden as it moves into the third millennium.

Why is it that the gardens of Versailles invite us to reflect on the passage of time more than the architecture? Why is it the slightest leaf, the tiniest blade of grass, rather than the marble statue, which incite inevitable thoughts about the brevity and meaning of life?

The garden is more fragile than any other work of art, always being weighed in the balance. A few years of loosening the grip, or abandoning the garden, can disfigure it for ever, as experience has shown. But over-enthusiastic or brutal intervention can leave scars which take a long time to heal. Gardening is a constant battle between disorder and order, the leaf and the gardener. The essence of its appeal and its ability to enchant us lies in the daily combat, like gains and losses made along a subtle and wavering line. Too little care can sap a garden's life, too much can rob it of its soul. The skill lies in maintaining a delicate balance between the two. Let us hope that those who come after us will not be less capable than those who came before, and that we shall not be either.

*The north arm of the Grand Canal*
*and the Bassin du Fer-à-cheval.*

# List of Illustrations

# Select Bibliography

Adams, William Howard *Les jardins de France*,
Éditions de l'Équerre, Paris, 1980

Babelon, Jean-Pierre, 'La restauration des jardins de Versailles',
in *Monumental No.4*, Direction du Patrimoine, Paris, 1993

Bellaigue, Raymonde de, *Le Potager du Roy*,
E.N.S.H., Versailles, 1982

Caffin-Carcy, Odile and Villard, Jacques, *Versailles et la Révolution*,
Éditions d'Art Lys, Versailles, 1988

Cayeux, Jean de, *Hubert Robert et les jardins*,
Herscher, Paris, 1987

Constans, Claire, *Versailles, château de la France et orgueil des rois*,
Gallimard-R.M.N., Paris, 1989

Desjardins, Gustave, *Le Petit Trianon*,
Éditions L. Bernard, Versailles, 1885

Dezallier d'Argenville, A.J., *La théorie et la pratique du jardinage*,
Mariette, Paris, 1747 edition

Feray, Jean, '*La Statuaire de Versailles*', Friends of V.M.F. Conference,
Versailles, 1993

Francastel, Pierre, *La création du Musée Historique de Versailles*,
Éditions Léon Bernard, Versailles, 1930

Friedman, Ann, 'The evolution of the Parterre d'eau',
in *The Journal of Garden History*, London, 1988

Ganay, Ernest de, *Les jardins en France*,
Librairie Larousse, Paris, 1949

Hazlehurst, F. Hamilton, *Gardens of Illusion*,
Vanderbilt University Press, Nashville, 1980

Heitzmann, Annick, 'Les jardins du Petit Trianon',
in *Les jardins de Versailles et de Trianon*, exhibition catalogue,
R.M.N., Paris, 1992

Hoog, Simone, '*Manière de montrer les jardins de Versailles par Louis XIV*
R.M.N., Paris, 1992

*Les jardins de Versailles et de Trianon d'André Le Nôtre à Richard Mique*,
exhibition catalogue, Château de Versailles, R.M.N. Paris, 1992

Lablaude, Pierre-André, 'Restauration et régénération de l'architecture
végétale du jardin de Versailles',
in *Monumental No. 4*, Direction du Patrimoine, Paris, 1993

La Quintinye, Jean-Baptiste de, *Instruction pour les jardins fruitiers et potagers*,
David, Paris, 1716 edition

Ledoux-Lebard, Denise, *Le Petit Trianon*,
Les Éditions de l'Amateur, Paris, 1989

Mariage, Thierry, *L'univers de Le Nôtre*,
Pierre Mardaga, Brussels, 1990

Marie, Alfred and Jane, *Naissance de Versailles*,
Éditions Vincent, Fréal et Cie, Paris, 1978

Montclos, Jean-Marie Pérouse de, *Versailles*,
Éditions Mengès, Paris, 1991

Nolhac, Pierre de, *Trianon*,
Éditions Louis Conard, Paris, 1927

*Projets pour Versailles, Dessins des Archives Nationales*,
exhibition catalogue, Archives Nationales, Paris, 1985

Taylor-Leduc, Susan B., 'The replantation of Versailles in the 18th century',
in *The Journal of Garden History*, London, 1992

Verlet, Pierre, *Le château de Versailles*,
Éditions Fayard, Paris, 1961-85

*Versailles vu par les peintres de Demachy à Lévy-Dhurmer*,
exhibition catalogue, Musée Lambinet, Versailles, 1992

Weber, Gérold, *Brunnen und Wasserkünste in Frankreich im Zeitalter von
Louis XIV*, Werner'sche Verlaggesellschaft, 1985

Colour separation : La Cromolito, Milan

Printed and bound by Graphiche Alma, Milan